# FRIENDS *of the*
## Livingston Public Library

### Gratefully Acknowledges
### the Contribution of

## Wendy & Gary Lubin

**For the 2018-2019 Membership Year**

# MILLENNEAGRAM

the enneagram guide for discovering
your truest, baddest self

## HANNAH PAASCH

HarperOne
*An Imprint of* HarperCollins*Publishers*

HarperOne

HarperCollins books may be purchased for educational, business, or sales promotional use. For information, please email the Special Markets Depart-ment at SPsales@harpercollins.com.

FIRST EDITION

*Designed by William Ruoto with Lucy Albanese*
*Illustration on page xiv © Evgeniy Belyaev/Shutterstock*

Library of Congress Cataloging-in-Publication Data

Names: Paasch, Hannah, 1990– author.

Title: Millenneagram : the enneagram guide for discovering your truest, baddest self / Hannah Paasch.

Description: First edition. | New York, NY : HarperCollins Publishers, [2019]

Identifiers: LCCN 2018045948 | ISBN 9780062872395 (hardcover)

Subjects: LCSH: Enneagram. | Personality.

Classification: LCC BF698.35.E54 P33 2019 | DDC 155.2/6—dc23

LC record available at https://lccn.loc.gov/2018045948

19 20 21 22 23   WOR   10 9 8 7 6 5 4 3 2 1

To the artists and activists,

The doers and shapers,

The makers and caretakers,

To the young,

The poor,

The tired,

The queer,

The seeking but never finding,

The fighting and never quitting,

This is for you.

May your foundation be firm,

Your self secure,

And your aim be true.

# CONTENTS

## PART III · THE THINKING TRIAD · 147

# GREETINGS AND SALUTATIONS

SELF-HELP BOOKS ABOUND. I SWEAR, EVERY DAY I SEE SOME new fix-it guide to getting your life back on track. As a connoisseur of inspiration—I love a good meaty *Chicken Soup for the Soul*, honey—I can tell you: most of them are gonna say the same old shit and just repackage it. Are there a few useful tidbits? Probably. Does it apply to you personally in any way? Probably not.

Enter the Enneagram.

Plainly put, the Enneagram is a personality typology that has a sneaky way of reflecting our innermost selves. Each personality type is given a number—there are nine types in total—but you should view that number as a starting point, not as a label to pigeonhole you.

Maybe it would help to start at the beginning. The Enneagram symbol itself is ancient, but the Enneagram model of human personalities as we understand it today is from a guy named Oscar Ichazo, who was inspired by the expansive ideology of philosopher and teacher George Gurdjieff. Ichazo, also a philosopher, sorted nine distinct personality types out of Gurdjieff's spiritual system of the seven deadly sins, positing that we all have go-to passions, or coping mechanisms, that create recurring themes throughout our lives. For example, some people just can't shake that they're missing something everyone else has, and they're pretty fuckin' envious of those around them. (Hello, baby Fours, I see you.)

In the 1970s, famed psychiatrist Claudio Naranjo synthesized the Enneagram with modern psychology and called each of the types an "ego fixation." That's just a fancy term that means we all have systems of coping mechanisms that help us survive what comes our way in life, as well as assign value to ourselves.

Today, the Enneagram is a system for understanding the self that marries what we know about the mind and what we sense about the spiritual realm. Just like how humans are half animal and half spirit, half concrete and half abstract, half learned and half unique, with one foot planted on the earth and the other leaping toward the stars—the Enneagram seeks to make sense of the wild, painful, glorious lives we lead.

I've been an Enneagram nerd since I first discovered it ten years ago, in my former life as a maudlin youth at a conservative Bible college (more on that later). I still remember where I was when I discovered my number, because I got fucking pissed off. I was sitting in a Starbucks in downtown Chicago, reading an Enneagram book and trying to peg all my bland-ass seminary friends. I started in on the type Four chapter, and my first thought reading the description was *Damn, these folks suck*. Second thought? *Fuck. That's me, isn't it?* I slammed the book down on the table and broke into a really intense pensive window-staring sesh. How could *I* of all people be some self-centered individualist? ME, dramatic? ME, tortured? AS IF.

When you read the words that call your bluff, everything changes.

After I'd come to terms with being a Four and read every book I could get my hot little hands on about it, I was able to laugh at my ego fixations (that shit hates being laughed at, lemme tell you what) and chart a path forward, smoothing out brain ruts and old emotional wounds as I went. I was able to figure out why the fuck I was so annoyed with my closest friends, which made me feel less crazy, while learning a deeper, driving sense of compassion that defined my interactions with them going forward.

The Enneagram helped me figure my shit out. I'm gonna show you how it can help you too.

## SO, HERE'S THE PITCH

Why should you care about an ancient personality typology whose origins are murky and can hardly be backed up by scientific data?

To borrow a line from our lord and savior Lin-Manuel Miranda (in *Hamilton*), we are "young, scrappy, and hungry," and we live in some goddamn terrifying times—times that require our presence, our intelligence, our intuition, and our wholeness. The Enneagram is a map to help us arrive at the unique version of wholeness possible for each of us. Only from this position, rootedness in who we are, what we believe, and what kind of story we are writing, will we be able to act bravely for the sake of justice and humanity, to approach our fucked-up world with the grounded courage it asks of us.

The Enneagram doesn't want to just slap a label on you and call it a day. The Enneagram is here to help you figure out where the fuck you are currently and where the fuck you want to go. Once you have these two key tidbits of information, you can start mapping the story you want to tell with your life. Ultimately, you don't need to worry about what you do—worry about the "why" behind it. The Enneagram is not about behavior modification; it's about motivations, fears, and basic desires. Deep shit.

What are the nine Enneagram personality types? Practitioners use different names for each one, emphasizing a different, but related, element. Here are some traditional type names:

**ONES: THE PERFECTIONIST, OR THE REFORMER**

**TWOS: THE HELPER, OR THE GIVER**

**THREES: THE ACHIEVER, OR THE PERFORMER**

**FOURS: THE ROMANTIC, OR THE INDIVIDUALIST**

**FIVES: THE INVESTIGATOR, OR THE OBSERVER**

**SIXES: THE LOYALIST, THE DEVIL'S ADVOCATE, OR THE QUESTIONER**

**SEVENS: THE ENTHUSIAST, THE EPICURE, OR THE ADVENTURER**

**EIGHTS: THE CHALLENGER, THE ASSERTER, OR THE BOSS**

**NINES: THE PEACEMAKER, OR THE MEDIATOR**

But it's a new era, with new ways of talking and thinking about identity. I hereby give you the Millenneagram:

## MILLENNEAGRAM ONES: THE MACHINE

## MILLENNEAGRAM TWOS: THE PARENT

## MILLENNEAGRAM THREES: THE WINNER

## MILLENNEAGRAM FOURS: THE TORTURED ARTIST

## MILLENNEAGRAM FIVES: THE DETECTIVE

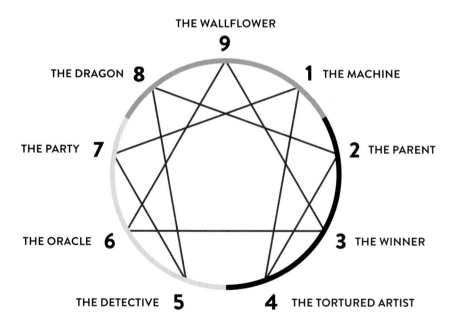

If you already know your type, I hope seeing it through the Millenneagram lens will help a little light bulb go off over your head. If you don't yet know your type, take a minute to flip to page xxviii for a short and sweet quiz to get you going.

Before we really get deep into it, though, you'll need to know a few terms. Allow me to be your tour guide.

## The Triads

The nine personality types are sorted into three triads: the Intuitive Triad, the Feeling Triad, and the Thinking Triad. You'll discover your triad in a hot sec, but your triad describes where your center of intelligence and guidance comes from. It also highlights both the source of your strength and the primary location of your ego fixation. Each triad is rooted in a part of the body: the Intuitive Triad's story takes place in the gut, the Feeling Triad's adventures play out in the heart, and the Thinking Triad's saga of loss and victory plays out in the brain. The Intuitive Triad includes Types Eight, Nine, and One, the Feeling Triad includes Types Two, Three, and Four, and the Thinking Triad includes Types Five, Six, and Seven. Sounds pretty melodramatic, I know, but another way to think about this is *Where does my power come from: the gut, the heart, or the brain?* For example, as a Four, I'm part of the Feeling Triad, which means the center of my strength and essence comes from my depth of feeling and emotional intelligence. Not to brag or anything.

I've chosen to highlight the triads because I've found they offer important info about the ruts we get stuck in, and I'm all about getting to the heart of shit. Why do we do what we do? What are we protecting ourselves from? What do our reactions tell us about what we value? I truly believe we cannot change the "what" without understanding the "why." Anything less is just behavior modification, and y'all better know right up front, I don't fuck with that shit.

## The Passions

Every number of the Enneagram is associated with a guiding passion, much like a cardinal sin, that can hijack the power of our true selves and use us as vehicles for its own nefarious ends. We often don't realize that we spend years in the service of an idea that is not entirely our own, and becoming aware of it can be alarming, if not downright depressing. I don't like the word "sin" because of the emotionally abusive connotations it carries for me (and many others), so for our purposes here in Millenneagram, I choose to use the word "passion" when describing the zombie-like adherence to one overarching need that each personality type can exhibit when not living through their own power.

For example, *I'm* fixated on the idea that other people have some important shit that helps them navigate the world and, ya know, be people, which I don't have. Most folks call that shit "envy." Being envious of normal people is this recurring theme in my life as a Four, and I set myself apart, creating an outsider complex that says, *I'm too unique for y'all. You wouldn't get it.*

We all are driven by these passions, and I'll unpack what each type's particular passion is so you can start to take your power back.

## Your Survival Story

Another piece we'll dig into is your survival story, which is how you got here. You use your ego fixations—your coping mechanisms and the recurring themes in your life—to write your survival story. Mine, for example, is that I'm a missionary kid, and as such, I'm an outsider—nobody really gets me, and I have to accept that. I've had a little chip on my shoulder about it for most of my life, and I've held friends and lovers at a distance in order to keep that story alive.

What have you written so far? As the author of your life, you get to decide where the adventure takes you. Unfortunately, a lot of us write plotlines that just keep us trudging through the same vicious cycles for years.

You have to reckon with your survival story before you can write new chapters and embark on new adventures. That's what this book is for.

## Integration and Disintegration

Now let's talk about two big, fancy words: integration and disintegration. Because each of us is a living document, moving and fluid and changing, each type has a direction of integration (where we head in times of stability) and disintegration (where we head in times of stress). Stability, crisis, stability, crisis—it's a vicious fucking cycle, huh? The key thing is to build the kind of brain habits in times of stability that will keep you fighting through the times of crisis. Identifying those processes in your life can help you take back control.

### Integration

In the words of Jonathan Van Ness, head groomer of *Queer Eye* and chief queen of my heart, THIS IS INTEGRATION STATION, HENNY. Integration refers to where a type always goes when they're healthy, i.e., what each personality type looks like when they're in a solid place. The masters of the Enneagram mapped out what this looks like, and I'll try to translate that information for you in true Garbage Oprah fashion so it can be accessible.

A healthy Two (the Parent) will integrate to a Four (the Tortured Artist), and as they do so, they redirect some of the energy they typically expend on others on themselves, which means they prioritize their own health and well-being and release their martyr complex a bit. A healthy Seven (the Party) will integrate to a Five (the Detective) and dig into their current interests instead of always trying on new ones. You might have noticed that integration often refers to a moment of *growth*. Mull that over for a while.

Integration happens only when you allow yourself to be vulnerable. And being vulnerable is hard and scary, especially for marginalized folks. Queer folks, like me, as well as people of color have been putting up with the material, physical, and emotional damage of the white supremacist cisheteropatriarchy for, like, ever. There're a lot of situations you shouldn't be vulnerable in, and nobody should demand that of you. But the Enneagram offers you a safe place to be vulnerable, and that place is with your self. Presence is the best and hardest gift you can give yourself.

It's key to note here that people who aren't white, straight, and cisgender are often just trying to survive, and any kind of self-helpy nonsense isn't always high on their priority list, for obvious reasons. I mean, *Hi, Maslow's hierarchy of needs!* People working on just getting by may not be super pressed about deep and nuanced internal work because, quite frankly, they don't have the bandwidth. However, the times we live in require activism, attention, compassion, and perhaps most importantly, self-love. While the political and social climate of our day seeks to assimilate us, it has never been more important to assert and affirm our value to the world. In order to get anybody else's oxygen mask on, we have to handle our own first. Integration is a big old giant leap in that direction.

### Disintegration

Disintegration is the direction we go when we're a wee bit spiraling. It's not something to fear or avoid but an important transition we can choose to catalyze into positive energy . . . or not. When a Two (the Parent) disintegrates to an Eight (the Dragon), they're finally able to express and display their anger, and to take back their agency from situations that are no longer feeding them. Disintegration can make you feel like a bit of a train wreck for a while, but crisis is not failure. It's evolution. Metamorphosis.

I'll walk you through some disintegration signs to look out for and how to observe those signs without judgment. It really does you no good to punish yourself for not being healthy. You can learn to pay attention to what disintegration provides and chart better paths forward for yourself. Sometimes ya gotta look a crisis right in the eyeballs and upset the order of your life to free up the building blocks to make something better.

## The Wings

To further nail down what the fuck your deal is, once you determine your type, you'll figure out if you have a "wing." Not everyone has a super-pronounced wing, but almost everyone has one they lean into from time to time. Your wing gives nuance to the decisions you make and the ways in which other people perceive you, plus it directs how you navigate the wants and needs of your base type.

A wing is one of the numbers next to your type—so as a Four (the Tortured Artist), I may have a Three wing (the Winner) or a Five wing (the Detective). A Three wing may make a Four more performative, outwardly directed, and, if I could just drag myself a quick sec, foolhardy. A Three wing is prone to big gestures and big decisions. A Five wing, on the other hand, may make a Four more melancholy, reclusive, thoughtful, concerned with researching the hell out of their interests, and—dare I say it—prone to procrastination.

The numbers on either side of your type are the only two options, okay? None of this Two-wing-Seven nonsense I've noticed some people trying to make into a thing. That's a hard nope. A lot of times we'll exhibit the traits of one wing until some formative life experience causes us to shift toward the other one. Again, being a person is a fluid fucking thing, and the Enneagram, of all the personality typologies, gives you room to breathe and to evolve.

Each chapter in this book will have a dedicated section to that type's wings.

## Instinctual Variants

"Instinctual variants" is an extra-psychey phrase to describe the area of life you fixate on the most—what I call subtypes. There are three subtypes: Self-Preserving, Social, and Sexual. Don't get too excited here, okay? We all know you're a horny shit-baby. Let me explain.

In *The Enneagram of Passions and Virtues*, Enneagram teacher Sandra Maitri gets to the heart of the matter when she says a

Self-Preserving subtype fixates on survival, a Social subtype fixates on belonging, and a Sexual subtype fixates on intimacy. At some point in your journey of existing, you may have felt wanting in one of these areas, and you learned to focus on it because you weren't getting enough nourishment and affirmation.

Self-Preserving subtypes are mostly concerned with the pragmatic aspects of life—getting what they need, when they need it, and creating the right physical space to feel safe and cared for.

Social subtypes make community their priority. These people seek to be influential and make a difference or to support, help, and engage with those around them, building a support system they can wrap around themselves like a snuggly safety blanket.

Sexual subtypes aren't just concerned with actual sex (although isn't everything about sex a little bit?) but with individual relationships, that good old one-on-one shit, focusing on best friends and partners, and having one or two confidants in their corner they can call their People with a capital *P*.

As it turns out, your survival story is based on the chapters of your life you've already written and those that have been written for you, a curious blend of nature and nurture that you're probably at least partially aware of. The variants will show up as threads woven throughout your tapestry. You'll begin to untangle them for yourself when we go into more detail about the variants in each chapter.

## THE AGE OF MILLENNEAGRAM

Let's pause for a sec to talk about the elephant in the room.

For some of you, you think Enneagram and you think about your preachy old church's youth group leader who got really into this shit and yelled about it from the pulpit one Sunday and immediately started typing every fucking body he came into contact with. The Enneagram got popular in Christian circles at some point, and now lots of people have a zealous cousin who posts about how she is "such a Two," with photos of Enneagram guidebooks alongside devotional Instagram pics of her Bible and latte. At least, that's been my experience.

Kids, listen up. If you're using, or want to use, the Enneagram for spiritual development, GREAT. I believe it can be a tool to deepen you, center you, and connect you to spiritual realities. But for many of us—the upstart activists, the queer kids, the visionaries and bohemians, the world changers—this whole system is about seeing our true selves and celebrating whoever the fuck that turns out to be.

That's why we're renaming this shit. Enter Millenneagram.

The Millenneagram is for those of us who believe that compassion and justice spring up from a centered, rooted self. It's for those of us who are grounded in vulnerability, in truth, and in a deep love of the world and ourselves.

## WHAT BRINGS YOU TO THIS PRACTICE TODAY?

There's something yoga teachers say at the beginning of a practice that I lowkey hate because it's so good and so unnerving. "Reflect on what brings you to practice today," they say. "What is your purpose?" *Oh god, I don't know*, I always think. I scramble to come up with something meaningful, something that isn't "My friend dragged me here" or "I don't know. I wanna bikini bod." Even though I'm often unable to answer this question myself, I now ask it of you.

What brings you to this practice today? Why are you reading this book? Is it to rediscover a sense of identity that feels missing? Is it to acquire a more expansive sense of self-love? Is everybody doing the Enneagram thing and you had to jump on the bandwagon? Hell, is it just to "get" your boyfriend's bullshit better? (Dump him, henny.) Regardless of what brings you here today, I'm grateful you came.

Chances are, you're fighting some hard battles. Perhaps you feel like nobody understands them but you. Chances are, you've survived some shit, and you've grown cold or hard or fearful because of it. That's okay too. However you arrived at this practice is okay. This is some come-as-you-are shit here, honey. The goal is to uncover your survival stories, honor them for getting you this far, and then compassionately release them so you can write new scripts for your future.

Here's what you're not gonna do: You will not use this book to make a list of all that is wrong about yourself and then punish yourself for all your wrong things. We're all a little fucked up, okay? Deal with it. Shaming yourself, aside from doing jack shit to actually help you integrate, is counterproductive, because the lie your number tells you, out of which most of your questionable behavior is born, is actually an important piece of the puzzle that is your wholeness.

Have you ever pulled some royal bullshit—just magnificently screwed with your life or your love or your job or something—and all of a sudden you learned something deeply true about yourself that you didn't previously know? When your emotional or spiritual back is against a wall, when you're lashing out and reacting and throwing a goddamn hissy fit, that right there is critical information. Observe that shit without judgment. How did you get there? What triggered this objectively childish nonsense?

The time and the effort you're willing to invest in self-discovery will decide how far along you get in the integration process. Ya get what ya pay for! It's a big-ass task, but it's good work worth doing. You gotta wade through your own muck to set a new course.

Buckle up. Here's why you're going on this journey:

*You'll hate people . . . less.*
I know, tall order. Everybody sucks. BUT I believe it was my good ole buddy Mr. Rogers who said something like there isn't anyone you can't love if you know their story, and I mostly agree. At the root of every person's story are the fears and motivations that propelled them in their life. Once you

know what those are, once you can get at the why behind the bullshit people we both love and tolerate inflict on us, it'll be easier to believe that the primary point of their existence is not to make you miserable.

*You'll learn how to chart new paths.*
A lot of us think old dogs can't learn new tricks, and that is some premium grade-A bullshit, y'all. I guarantee your mind wants to learn new things. You want to go new places. Your true self is gasping for air. With the Enneagram, you can become aware of the puppet strings your ego has tied you up with and use them as leads instead to thoughtfully maneuver yourself forward. You're nobody's Pinocchio, bitch. You're a real boy (or girl or nonbinary human) now.

*You'll start believing that YOU are the point of YOU.*
Hear me on this one. You are living the only life you get. You will play important roles in other lives, but this is the only one you get. This is the only body (that you know of). This is the only time. No pressure, but your life is happening now. All around you. It's time to quit phoning that shit in.

No matter what brain ruts or coping mechanisms your personality has learned to rely on, you cannot lose you. Your essence is always there, nestled in your body, waiting for permission to come out and run around a bit. Acknowledge her now or acknowledge her later, she'll still be there, waiting.

It's your time to jump in, friends. Listen, I know you like shit handed to you, but the truth is that finding out your number is kind of a little self-discovery journey. Yes, there's a quiz next to find out your type, but look for other Enneagram-based quizzes and take a few more to see what feels right. No one test can tell you exactly what your type is. At the end of the day, the type that punches you in the gut and runs off with your purse is you, boo.

Remember, you are the point of you. You have just a few hours, a few days, strung together like paper links in a chain, a few precious years to live, to fuck, to laugh, to build, to love, and to fight. This is it.

Babes and trolls,

Kids and queers,

We have gathered here today to change.

We are here to climb our mountains, to face our demons, to write new adventures. Let's dig ourselves out of our goddamn ditches together.

# MILLENNEAGRAM
## QUIZ*

1.  **When someone asks for your advice, you:**

    a.  hit 'em with your gut instrict.

    b.  answer based on your emotional knowledge of yourself and the asker.

    c.  think it over and then respond with your rational brain.

2.  **You would be most upset if . . .**

    a.  you had no control over yourself or the shit around you.

    b.  your babe or your BFF misunderstood you.

    c.  you couldn't get enough information to make an informed decision for your life.

3.  **You are driven by . . .**

    a.  feeling gloriously independent. You don't like feeling reliant on something or someone else.

---

\*  Do not base your entire Millenneagram experience off this quiz. I'm getting you in the ballpark; I'm not diagnosing you, 'kay? If you want to take more complex quizzes, I've hooked you up with a list of resources at the back of the book.

b.   getting along with everyone. You'll stay up at night if you've had a minor misunderstanding with someone.

c.   being informed. You like to be the person your friends come to when they need the best restaurant recommendation or best mechanic in town.

**4.   You get off on . . .**

a.   knowing what the right thing is, and then doing it.

b.   feeling like people see you for who you really are.

c.   learning new shit and stockpiling knowledge and experiences to prepare yourself for life and the world.

**5.   What keeps you up at night is . . .**

a.   frustration. You think about something you or someone around you did wrong, and you can't let go of it.

b.   embarrassment. You spin your wheels going over something that happened that humiliated you.

c.   anxiety. You can't stop thinking about what's going to happen tomorrow.

If you answered (a) on two or more questions, skip to **THE INTUITIVE TRIAD**.

If you answered (b) on two or more questions, skip to **THE FEELING TRIAD**.

If you answered (c) on two or more questions, skip to **THE THINKING TRIAD**.

# THE INTUITIVE TRIAD

**1.   You would rather . . .**

a.   be in charge of your own destiny.

b.   be left in solitude to experience calm, peaceful bliss.

c.   be the absolutely best fucking version of yourself you are capable of being.

**2.   You are most afraid of . . .**

a.   someone daring to control you. Nice try, bitch.

b.   not being able to find a sense of balance. You're all about that calm headspace shit.

c.   setting a bad example. You hate to admit it, but you're a mad stickler for getting things done right.

**3.   You are happiest . . .**

a.   when you and your intuition are in perfect sync.

b.   chilling in the comfort of your own home.

c.   when someone lets you fix some shit that needs it badly.

**4.   You secretly just want . . .**

a.   TO PROTECT YOURSELF AND THE FOLKS YOU LOVE. IS THAT SO MUCH TO ASK?

b.   a little peace and quiet . . . and snacks.

c.   to do what you like, the way you like it, and fucking crush it.

5. **People rely on you for . . .**

   a. unleashing righteous hell when necessary.

   b. a cozy getaway from the category 5 hurricane of life.

   c. grade-A premium life advice.

If you answered (a) on two or more questions, you're probably an **EIGHT**.

If you answered (b) on two or more questions, you're probably a **NINE**.

If you answered (c) on two or more questions, you're probably a **ONE**.

If you find that your results point you toward two different types, read the chapters about each one to get a better sense of which is you.

# THE FEELING TRIAD

1. **You would rather be seen as . . .**

   a. helpful, needed, and taking care of people. You always have a snack in your bag just in case, you know?

   b. successful. You're kicking ass and taking names.

   c. unique. You're a fucking snowflake and the world is lucky to have you.

**2.  You are most afraid of . . .**

    a.    not being needed. You are Mrs. Weasley to a T.

    b.    not achieving your goals. Like, just work harder. What's the problem here?!

    c.    not finding your purpose. You're just so DEEP and have so much to EXPLORE about yourself and your UNIQUE contribution to the world.

**3.  You are happiest when you . . .**

    a.    feel you belong and are loved—*HUGS*.

    b.    are fucking crushing it in life.

    c.    have a free day in the art shed to express your creativity.

**4.  You secretly just want . . .**

    a.    to be there for literally everyone always. JK—you just love being the NICE person who is RELIABLE and INDISPENSIBLE.

    b.    world domination. JK, but for real: Is this a networking opportunity? Can you make any connections here?

    c.    TO BE A "REAL" ARTIST. JK—you're just going to talk about writing poems in a bar and throw back gin and tonics. . . . Are you Kerouac yet?

**5.  People rely on you for . . .**

    a.    that favor no one else will do. (Be honest, how many times have you helped someone move?)

b. savvy business advice, obvi.

c. creative inspiration (DRINK in the VIBES).

If you answered (a) on two or more questions, you're probably a **TWO**.

If you answered (b) on two or more questions, you're probably a **THREE**.

If you answered (c) on two or more questions, you're probably a **FOUR**.

If you find that your results point you toward two different types, read the chapters about each one to get a better sense of which is you.

# THE THINKING TRIAD

1. **You would rather . . .**

   a. be an expert in a niche field (*pushes glasses up nose*).

   b. be loyal, dependable, and consistent as fuck.

   c. check off all the amazing ADVENTURES on your bucket list.

2. **You are most afraid of . . .**

   a. not having enough information to solve all life's problems. You've read an article about how that happens sometimes.

b.   not being able to avoid complete and utter disaster. You'll be right back—you just want to make *sure* you unplugged your hair dryer.

c.   pausing long enough to reckon with what's actually going on in your feelings. LA, LA, LA—you're not listening, too busy inviting literally everyone out tonight to have a GOOD TIME.

**3.   You are happiest . . .**

a.   in a library, unbothered (*licks thumb and turns page*).

b.   having a glass of wine surrounded by your carefully vetted community of select, trustworthy friends.

c.   on a dance club floor three drinks in with no ride home.

**4.   You secretly just want . . .**

a.   mastery of a difficult but useful topic. Friday nights curled up with a documentary are your jam.

b.   a sure thing. You just want people and things to be dependable and safe. Is that too much to ask?

c.   a life of adventure worth writing books about. No FOMO for you—you never MISS OUT.

**5.   People rely on you for . . .**

a.   being a walking Wikipedia, Google, and concierge service who can provide hoards of information on the spot.

b.   thoughtful, incisive advice on the best path forward because you've already thought through every possible horrible scenario that could possibly happen.

c.   starting the party when you walk in.

If you answered (a) on two or more questions, you're probably a FIVE.

If you answered (b) on two or more questions, you're probably a SIX.

If you answered (c) on two or more questions, you're probably a SEVEN.

If you find that your results point you toward two different types, read the chapters about each one to get a better sense of which is you.

# HOW EACH TYPE TRAVELS BY AIRPLANE

### Ones

Group A1–30, bitches, read 'em and weep. I've been checked in for a week—don't ask how. Yes, all my liquids are in three-ounce bottles purchased for this express purpose.

### Fours

I'm gonna get to my gate two hours early so I can look plaintive and languid while people-watching over a glass of wine and write poetry about propellers or the journey of life or some shit.

### Sevens

Getting beers with my new friend I met in line at security. I complimented them on their sweet kicks, and here we are, kickin' it, being besties. Gonna vacation in Cabo together next spring, except not 'cause I'll forget.

## Twos

Hi, honey, where's your mom?
Oh my God, you're flying alone?
Not anymore, sweetheart.
Mommy's here! I mean, she's not,
but I am, and we're going to have
a great time. Oh, you just wanna
play with your Nintendo DS?
That's fine. I get it. I'll just sit here.

## Threes

How on point is my airport look?
I look fresh, fierce, and
professional, don't I?
Yes, my bomb shoes do match
my luggage, thanks for noticing.
Ya never know where you're
gonna meet your next career-
deciding connection.

## Fives

I was just reading up on statistics
about airplane deaths before we
got here. It's fine—we have a good
chance of survival. Here, since
you're a captive audience, let me
tell you all the things about
my recent all-encompassing,
very niche area of research.

## Sixes

Oh my God, okay, we're going to
be late. Oh my God, okay, we're
early. It's good, it's good, we're all
good. I hate flying so much. Like,
so many things could go wrong with
planes, you know? Like, I'm careening
through space on a CHAIR in
the SKY. How is that safe?

## Eights

ALL RIGHT, LISTEN, PEOPLE.
Here's the deal. Stay the
fuck together. I'll go buy the
sandwiches. Joey, where the fuck
is your passport? God, if you want
something done, you gotta
fucking do it yourself.

## Nines

I have downloaded eight movies
and sixteen audiobooks so
I can smile blandly at my
seatmates while not hearing them
over my headphones. Yes, I'm
wearing my house shoes onto this
plane right now. I'm boutta take
a fucking nap, am I not?

# THE INTUITIVE TRIAD

# PART I

# GUT FOLKS

## THE INTUITIVE TRIAD

### TYPES 8, 9, AND 1

Survival lies in sanity, and sanity lies in paying attention . . .
the capacity for delight is the gift of paying attention.

—JULIA CAMERON, *THE ARTIST'S WAY*

OUR MILLENNEAGRAM JOURNEY BEGINS WITH THE INTUITIVE
Triad. Imma call these kids gut folks, because the wisdom of the
body is often associated with the gut, and frankly, it's just more fun
to say.

If you're an Intuitive type—an Eight, Nine, or One—your primary source of wisdom is your body. Sounds a touch hippie-dippie—I get it—but hear me out. Intuitive types, at their core, their root, their truest self, know what needs to be done. They're the masters of right action.

Y'all are probably going to wonder why the hell the numbers are in this order, and Ones will wonder what is EVEN the point of numbers if they're not going to be in the correct freaking order?! The master Enneagram teachers have designated Three, Six and Nine as the center number in each of the triads, as they tend to embody the core struggles and strengths of each triad and draw the most consistently from the numbers on either side of them. So, for the Intuitive Triad, we've got Nines at the center, with Eights and Ones on either side. Just go with it, 'kay?

My little sis, Ames, is an Eight, and as such she always seems to be deeply prepared for every situation that comes her way in a manner I find legit disturbing. Like, HOW, BITCH? She works in an airport and is often required to handle the customers who are wilding out, drunk off their asses, or otherwise making a stink about how the thunderstorm in Miami fucked up their connection. Listen, if there was some dickhead hollering in my face about what a bitch I was for not fixing the weather, I would stand there like a deer in the goddamn headlights, y'all. A Thinking Triad type would probably disintegrate immediately after the reaction and declare the following day a "people-less" day. Ames, though, is on it. She is firm, she is direct, and she is dialing airport security with one hand while de-escalating the situation with her words. She intuitively understands exactly what the situation requires and how to manage it. If that's not a fucking superpower, I don't know what is.

Unfortunately, most people are pretty freaking disconnected from the key source of their individual power. Like, it's bad. The less healthy gut folks are, the less able they are to trust their own instincts. Repression comes into play here, as a means of self-protection. Their egos build imitations of their true power for them to lean on. This is what I like to call a "personality ledge," and it helps them wallflower it up, standing on the sidelines and sitting out of the dance of their own lives. You'll notice I often say that a lack of presence is at the core of what keeps us stuck in our brain ruts, because being present requires a level of vulnerability with ourselves that most of us just don't have. Yet.

At the base of the reactionary responses of most Intuitive types is what Don Richard Riso and Russ Hudson (founders of The Enneagram Institute and authors of *Personality Types* and *The Wisdom of the Enneagram*—aka my Enneagram dads) call a "resistance to reality." Essentially, these people feel the need to ward off the harmful effects of the world around them by taking an antagonistic or at least passively defiant approach to outside stimuli. There's a bit of an antagonistic mentality at play with these kids, like they're saying, "If I don't know what it is, it better stay way the hell away from me." The Feeling Triad types' knee-jerk reaction to new information or stimuli might be to tacitly accept something for the sake of saving face, and the Thinking Triad types might respond by doing anxious research, but Intuitive folks are like, *Nahhhh, man. Fuck that noise!* Each type in the triad responds differently, though, so let's take a look at each in turn.

## HOW EIGHTS FIT INTO THE INTUITIVE TRIAD

Instinctively powerful and righteously angry, Eights build aggressive and antagonistic reactions to the world while being out of touch with their own deep-rooted power. Eights then use this fake-ass aggro bullshit to write their survival stories. It works, but . . . yikes.

My dear friend Kevin puts it this way:

> Anger is a familiar friend of mine. It is the fire that sits at the base of my stomach that fuels all the work that I do. . . . When I first started my advocacy work, it was nothing for me to write a scathing blog post about a poor interaction I had with church folks or people in very close proximity to me. . . . An Eight knows how to craft a powerful and scathing statement that will eviscerate [someone's] sense of worth and ability. It's an Eight's way of maintaining a sense of control and making sure that no one can come too close.

Though we see it subtly in the other Intuitive types too, Eights are the poster children for this kind of flailing antagonism. Someone didn't do their job, usually a parental or nurturing figure, and the Eight at an early age had to come in and handle shit, to take the reins before they were quite ready. An Eight has never met a challenge they couldn't quickly rise to, but it remains a sore spot that they had to construct barriers to protect the small, tender kid inside them. Trying to get close to an Eight can be a trip, because the first sign of you trying to chip away at those barriers can send an Eight into full-blown attack mode, and you're gonna be the one obliterated, friend.

Freaked the fuck out about being controlled in any way, Eights try to set boundaries for their reality: "This is cool. This isn't." "This is unacceptable. This is okay." When Eights are divorced from their true selves, this reality managing—keeping the wrong shit out and the right shit in—is a full-time job.

Healthy Eights own their power and aren't super concerned about who could possibly challenge it. They know who they are, and if you don't, bitch, you boutta learn.

## HOW NINES FIT INTO THE INTUITIVE TRIAD

Nines are reality managers too, but they are most concerned about their equilibrium being upset by either internal or external forces. When they're disconnected from their true selves, they expend what little energy they have on intuitively keeping their boat unrocked by feelings or circumstances.

Unlike Eights, Nines often report having normal-ass or even happy childhoods, and there's a reason for this. They have a tendency to look back on the past with rose-colored glasses, blocking out the unpleasant in order not to experience it again. Although they also felt the need to assume adulthood long before they were ready, it was more of a gradual transition, as Nines received the vague but insidious message that they were kinda superfluous. That their opinions and their voice didn't matter. Nines played the role of peacekeeper, feeling like they had to step in and keep people away from each other's throats, and erasing their own wants and needs in favor of whatever would keep the peace. While some Nines lean toward the serious side of things, plenty are carefree and goofy, using humor as a way to diffuse tense situations—even if those tense situations are their own emotional landscapes. Laugh so you don't feel—am I right?!

Although they often get a reputation as a peacemaker (or peacekeeper), a seed of resentment was planted early on, and Nines can sit on that shit, stuffing and repressing their anger for years. Everything repressed ends up coming out at some point, though, and you can bet that your fave Nine, as chill as they may seem, will reach a boiling-over point someday—even if it's about nine years later than the rest of us would.

Healthy Nines are able to bring a sense of balance to their relationships and every situation they find themselves in—like, that shit rubs off. They're able to impart that stability and groundedness to everyone in their orbit, and let's be real: most of us need the hell out of that shit.

## HOW ONES FIT INTO THE INTUITIVE TRIAD

Where Eights direct their repressive energy outward, and Nines direct it both toward themselves and the world around them, Ones direct that hose mainly at their own house. Being a human is messy as fuck, and Ones aren't interested in all the shades of gray. Ones aim to manage primarily their own reality, as if they could perfect themselves by sheer force of will.

Any anger they feel, they direct at themselves, thinking that by suppression they will force themselves into the right shape, the right feelings, the right decisions, and the right thoughts. Think Aaron Burr from Lin-Manuel Miranda's play *Hamilton:* "I am the one thing in life I can control." While Ones are constantly taking note of everything that requires fixing in the world around them, passing judgment on the people, places, and systems they are confronted with, there is no one they pass more judgment on or seek more to change than themselves.

A healthy One blends their penchant for clarity with compassion, allowing them to communicate clearly with peers and loved ones without trampling them. These motherfuckers know how to pull a John Mayer and say what they need to say, and, boy, if we couldn't all learn a thing or two from that.

## A WAKE-UP CALL FOR MY INTUITIVE KIDS

Showing up faithfully for your life and your true self is hard-ass work, and you may not have anything to show for your endeavors for a while. It can be kind of embarrassing to look yourself in the eye after years of looking away. Yet for the Intuitive Triad folks, nothing could be more important.

What can seem, or even FEEL, like intuition often has more to do with the personality you've constructed than with the voice of your true self. Deciphering which is which is quite the task. My friend Corey, a One, calls it "working on essence." He says: "The hardest thing for a One is to be at home and content with themselves."

What's another word for that? Presence. For those in the Intuitive Triad, listening to the wisdom of your body requires stillness, curiosity, and presence—difficult gifts to give oneself in a world that is overrun with noise, movement, and the capitalist notion of constant productivity. Fuck productivity—am I right? The good shit, the best shit, takes time to percolate.

When you lose touch with your intuition, you end up losing

touch with your own needs, wants, and tenderness. So, gut folks, how do you get back in touch with your intuition? Be present. Get angry. As my queen Julia Cameron says in her seminal work *The Artist's Way* (which everyone should read if they have half a passion in their body): "Anger is fuel."[1] We often think about anger as an emotion, and one to be avoided at that. I want you to start thinking about your anger as energy. It's not a landing place. It's the gasoline that gets you to your next destination.

Cameron continues: "But we are *nice* people, and what we do with our anger is stuff it, deny it, bury it, block it, hide it, lie about it, medicate it, muffle it, ignore it. We do everything but *listen* it." I want you to see your anger, and its triggers, as a road map. When you feel it, you know something is not quite right, and it gives you the chance to ask yourself what that might be. People are so afraid of their anger being used negatively that they end up becoming their own self-fulfilling prophecy. If you ignore anger, it doesn't just disappear, honey. It hardens into bitterness, into resentment. We see this so clearly in the Nines, who stuff their anger down deep.

Anger requires action, and in order for you to act, you have to acknowledge that you really feel it. That it's really there. You cannot use anger as a cover-up for something else. You cannot avoid it or stuff it down. Preaching to the choir here, people.

---

1. Julia Cameron, *The Artist's Way* (Los Angeles: TarcherPerigee, 1992).

Cameron says that anger tells us we "can't get away with our old life any longer." Paying attention to your anger means you have to take action, and that's fucking hard. I get it. Anger means you cannot overlook the poor treatment you've been putting up with. Anger means you have to amend your life to fit the truest version of yourself. Anger means you have to feel and face your feelings, instead of taking them out on your loved ones or yourself.

Chances are that you had to grow up too fast, that you carry a lot of anger you either take out on the nearest unsuspecting victim, dissociate from, or actively repress. That's a lot of work, though, darling. You gotta be exhausted by now. You're spending all your precious time and energy and attention on NOT paying attention to yourself. Not to be a dick, but, like, that's a bad strategy, boo.

Let's activate that anger into right action. How 'bout it, honey?

# MILLENNEAGRAM
# 8

## THE DRAGON

"

Your muchness is a gift.

**JAMIE LEE FINCH**

I COULDN'T HEAR MUCH FROM WHERE I WAS HIDING IN MY bedroom closet, but what I could decipher was that shit was bad. Our trash landlord had shown up, unannounced, hollering things about broken leases, and I had immediately retreated. Like, fetal-position-in-the-closet retreated. My friend Emily knocked on the closet door and handed me a half-empty bottle of tequila.

"She's screaming at your landlord in the driveway," she told me somberly. "So I'd, uh, start drinking." I felt my face go white, and I tipped the dang bottle back. There wasn't a drunker bitch in Nashville that godforsaken night.

The "she" in question here was Caitlin, my Eight roommate, a woman whose capacity for fun was eclipsed only by her ferocity when cornered. Some days I was convinced she was some Stone Age carnivore reincarnated as a skinny ukulele-playing white girl with bangs and a chain-smoking habit.

Caitlin barged into my room moments later, her face flushed with rage but also a hint of excitement. *The thrill of the chase*, I thought gloomily.

"I told him that he doesn't get to fuck with my friends like that!" Caitlin announced. When we didn't immediately respond by thanking her or congratulating her on her win, the following pause hung heavy in the air. Then she huffed: "You know I was just protecting you two, right?"

*I could think of better ways than getting us evicted*, I thought, but I kept that to myself. You don't challenge a beast of prey who's just been in a death match. I both understood and resented the fact that, in her mind, escalating the situation was the price she had to pay for "protecting" us, her mild-mannered roommates who were mostly just tryna stay un-homeless. For Caitlin, protecting us from this perceived antagonist—our landlord—tapped into her core impulses as an Eight: she was confrontational, yes, but she also trusted her gut and followed her unwavering self-confidence.

My roommate, the Dragon.

## HERE BE DRAGONS

I call Eights Dragons because no other number possesses raw intuitive power on their level. Eights are larger than life, armed with a vivacious, magnetic intensity that follows them into every space, upsetting the power dynamics of a party and resetting its gravitational pull. They often have a sort of reactionary antagonism to every situation, expecting to be on the offensive and sometimes opposing shit just for the hell of it if it's new or they don't get it yet. Eights can step into any situation and sense who's in charge, and if that person in power isn't handling shit, they're more than willing to (read: definitely going to) take over. It's not that Eights necessarily have to be the center of attention—they largely leave the shenanigans up to the Sevens—but they carry a sense of power and authority that demands respect and deference. You can almost feel the energy shift when an Eight walks into the room.

Eights are leaders, protectors, people who take charge and are generally active in their spaces. They are pushers. They test the boundaries of any sphere in which they find themselves and expand any boundaries that are too restrictive. Like the dragons of the fairytales, they have the ability to burn shit to the ground, which, when harnessed appropriately, allows them to actively effect change like few other types can. Unfortunately, also like dragons, a lot of the time their bluster and antagonism may cause them to burn down shit that needed to stay standing.

## PASSION: LUST

Eights are connected to the cardinal passion of lust. No, not the kind you're thinking of, asshat. Get your damn brain outta the gutter! Lust can be sexual, but it also can be a driving, all-encompassing force pushing someone toward whatever makes them feel right or powerful. Unlike Threes, who are also often natural-born leaders and go-getters, Eights follow a compass entirely their own, unmoved by and sometimes downright antagonistic toward any opinions except their own.

Lust is a funny thing, because at first glance it seems expansive, energizing, and disconnected from attachment. Exercising it looks like reclaiming one's power in the world. Unfortunately, for the less healthy Eights, lust becomes an unquenchable need, disconnecting them from the present and dragging them toward the next mountain to climb or challenge to overcome. Ain't no mountain high enough for these kids.

## SURVIVAL STORY: FOLLOW YOUR HEART

Being a part of the Intuitive Triad, a Millenneagram Eight is the original follow-your-heart bitch. She realized early on that plodding along and following other people's rules was not the best-case scenario for her happiness, and some unlucky somebody somewhere pushed her just a hair too far. If she were to follow any plan that wasn't her own, she would be settling somehow, and a follow-your-heart bitch will have none of that.

We hear "follow your heart" and think unicorns and stardust. Hardly. Following your heart means renouncing the expectations that family, religion, and culture impose on you, which is some tough-ass shit. Eights know they need every weapon in their arsenal to rise to the task: their pragmatism, their leadership, their assertiveness, and just a touch of riot fire. To turn your wish into the world's command, you have to be able to forge ahead into every situation that presents itself and be like "I've got this. Mischief managed."

## THE FUCK-IT MOMENT

I bet if you asked just about any Eight, they could recall the exact moment in their lives when the gears switched. At some formative point, your friendly neighborhood Eight just had it UP TO HERE and finally decided they weren't letting anyone else decide shit for them from there on out. I call it the "fuck-it moment." Most of us sit around waiting for someone to give us permission to change, to expand, to grow. Eights don't wait for anyone to tell them they're allowed to move in the direction of their wants and needs. This is what sets an Eight apart from the rest of us. This fuck-it moment puts them on a new trajectory—one in which they, rather than a parent figure or a church or the expectations of their community, are calling the shots. They actively choose to be the protagonists in their story.

I remember my baby sister's fuck-it moment clearly, because it shook my understanding of the accepted order of things.

Ames and I shared just about everything: a bedroom, our friends,

our secrets, the whole nine. There was a reason for our closeness—
we were largely insulated from the world's watchful eye because we
were the obnoxious triple threat of being missionary kids, pastor's
kids, and homeschooled. This meant that for my parents to keep
their jobs, our family had to look and behave a certain way. Righteous. Blameless. I, of course, internalized this accepted order of
things and became a mad secretive bitch, playing along the best that
my burgeoning existential angst and depressive symptoms would
allow.

One day, when Ames and I were twelve and thirteen, respec-
tively, I wandered into Amy's room and saw her holding a small
jewelry box, which held a glittering silver strand with a pendant on
the end, the sort of thing a not-quite-teenage girl doesn't tend to
have lying around.

"Amy!" I gasped. "What IS that and where did you get it?!"

"Elliot gave it to me," she said plainly, looking me dead in the
eyes. Her look felt like a dare. Elliot?! The church crush who wasn't
allowed to be seen talking to Amy for more than five minutes before
the Youth Group Purity Squad was unleashed?! The drama! The
audacity! The hot goss of it all!

"Amy," I said seriously, after a moment's silent reflection on this
fantastic but dangerous turn of events, "you can't tell anybody about
this. You know we're not allowed to date anybody, and it'll look
wrong. Also like, mom and dad are def taking that away."

She looked nonplussed, so I pressed.

"You know this, right?"

She paused, and there was riot fire behind her dark blue eyes.

"You know what?" she barked. "I'm gonna tell whoever I want, I'm gonna keep it, and I . . . don't . . . CARE." I didn't know it at the time, but this was her fuck-it moment. A Dragon was born.

I whole-ass gasped. Who did my little fucking sister think she was, eschewing tradition AND expectation in one imperious, momentary decision? A queen?! Britney Spears?! A Spice Girl?! (This was the '00s, after all.) I was furious but also mad jealous of the balls she had suddenly acquired, seemingly out of thin air. Why didn't I have that kind of pluck? I would spend the next decade asking myself that same question before I happened upon any of my own.

Turns out you can't order pluck on Amazon, but if you hang out with an Eight long enough, some moxie just might rub off. Consider it their fairy dust.

## WINGS

The two wings for the Eight are the Seven (the Party) and the Nine (the Wallflower). The Seven wing and the Nine wing bring very distinct energies to the Eight power, strongly influencing how the

Eight is perceived by peers, coworkers, etc. An Eight with a Seven wing (also noted as 8w7) has the Eight intensity but with a heavy, almost deceptive dose of fun that masks their natural antagonism and defensiveness.

8w7s are larger than fucking life, strategically extra, moderators and instigators of both fun-having and necessary conflict. They seem to have a need to keep up with themselves, to compete with their own previous successes, parties, and general shenanigans. While you may be having the time of your life with them, you can't help wondering from time to time whether something else is going on under the surface of the fun—some agenda quietly being furthered while you're throwing back shots. On the surface, 8w7s are rarely visibly moved or cowed by would-be competitors, although they can get lowkey fixated on them in private and plot very elaborate and dramatic demises for their foes and frenemies. The petty runs deep, my friends!

Often read as Sevens, 8w7s are big planners and big dreamers, enlisting some of the charm of Threes to sell their schemes to assistants, volunteers, and donors. Their confidence is legendary, and their pitches are too. 8w7s are never-back-down bitches. When push comes to shove, these kids are gonna *shove*, if ya know what I mean. An 8w7 will eviscerate your shit, reinsert their earrings, and get right back to enjoying their evening, sans you. An 8w7 headed toward integration is charismatic and vulnerable, powerful and tender. They often continue to take on and launch big-picture endeavors, but with a groundedness that comes from living and breathing and moving out of the wisdom of their body.

The Nine wing, however, brings a significant helping of "can't be bothered" to the Eight's usual presence and prowess. An 8w9 resents having to be ON all the time, since there's so much fuckery in the world that they feel is their responsibility to handle, and honestly, how dare the world be constantly creating more of it all the time? The Nine wing also lends a seriousness to the Eight, an over-attention to detail, and an intimidating calm. An 8w9 is adept at projecting precisely the amount of interest they have in connecting with you and are used to people adhering to the boundaries they set in place.

8w9s are far lower on the party-animal spectrum than their charismatic counterparts, the 8w7s, although given the right circumstances—which they rigidly prescribe—they can occasionally let their hair down. 8w9 millennials often give off a "twenty-five going on forty" vibe, like the idea of lightening up has never occurred to them. The healthier they get, the more able they are to allow the dear, tenderhearted kid they've been protecting all these years to sneak out for love, affection and fun every now and then—but only with very carefully selected individuals or in situations where they feel most in tune with their power. As Eights lean into the deep knowing of their gut wisdom, they can create an atmosphere of balance and control wherever they go—whether that's a sweaty club dance floor or the quiet of their own bedroom.

## INSTINCTUAL VARIANTS

### Self-Preserving Eights

Riso and Hudson describe the Self-Preserving Eight as the quintessential "survivor."[1] More reserved and focused than the other subtypes, the Self-Pres Eight often experiences a lack of some kind in their youth that they try to fill as an adult. Underneath the bravado of the Eight is the small child they used to be, and now it's their job to protect and parent the way they weren't. A Self-Pres Eight isn't so much concerned with keeping up appearances or politeness if that gets in the way of a goal. Essentially, imagine every grisly protagonist in an apocalypse movie—brave, gruff, getting shit done, and handling shit. There's your Self-Pres Eight.

### Social Eights

Social Eights are more concerned about the relationships that surround them than Self-Pres Eights are. They invest a ton in the

---

1. Don Richard Riso and Russ Hudson, *The Wisdom of the Enneagram* (New York: Bantam, 1999).

people they care about, but they're hypervigilant about honor and trust, and they'll tell you what the fuck is up if you cross one of their boundaries. An Eight's memory is long, believe you me. They will not easily forget a fuck-up—not for any particularly petty reason, but primarily because, well, you have been tried, tested, and found wanting. (Miss you, Heath Ledger.)

Social Eights have a direct connection with Twos (especially Twos in disintegration) because they assume the role of protective parent if they sense any kind of predator encroaching on their "pack." We're talking alpha-wolf shit here. Social Eights pay less attention to their own needs and spend more of their time and energy on making sure everyone around them is settled and cared for.

## Sexual Eights

Sexual Eights are the most obviously rebellious of the three subtypes: they are loud, they are expressive, and they did not fucking come to play! These Eights draw every eye to them when they walk into a room (a Seven wing complements this energy nicely). They're often considered the energetic center of a circle they find themselves in. Sexual Eights also put a greater emphasis on one or two intimate relationships, and they go to those people for practically everything. Eights don't like having needs, and they certainly don't like letting other people meet these needs, so if a Sexual Eight chooses to accept help from you, you're in it for the long haul, my friend.

## ACCESSING THE TEDDY BEAR: INTEGRATION
## AND DISINTEGRATION FOR THE EIGHT

At their healthiest, an Eight integrates to a Two. Remember, integration means growth in the direction of stability. Eights integrate to Two, and Twos disintegrate—regress and revert to when stressed—to Eight, so I like to think of the Eight-Two continuum as the good cop, bad cop routine. Both Eights and Twos naturally take on a parental role with the people closest to them, conflicted by the need to help and the need to control. They're often co-occurring instincts, aren't they? (We'll talk more about Two disintegration in the Two chapter, never you fret.) When Eight goes to Two, they lean into all the generosity and bigheartedness their true self has to offer, and they offer their powerful assistance freely. This is the motherfucker you want on your team. Their combined kindness and ferocity makes them anyone's A-Team gladiator. She's gonna go to the mats for you, quitting is not an option, etc., etc.

When an Eight disintegrates, they go to Five, retreating into their minds and feeling suddenly unprepared to meet the world with their signature power. Stress builds and the super-confident and self-assured Eight is unable to move—like someone suddenly cut them off at the knees. Retreating from the world, for a stressed Eight, is about both licking wounds and re-strategizing. They think if they ruminate long enough on their next best move, essentially planning out steps like an embattled army trying to recover post-ambush, they suddenly will find the power they've misplaced. These kids are like the Stark family in *Game of Thrones*—powerful as fuck but constantly pulling the short end of the stick, losing key players, and retreating in desperation.

Eights at this stage of stress struggle to see anything clearly—it's as if they suddenly approach life with dirty glasses on, and they can't seem to sufficiently wipe them clean. They don't want people to see them like this, so they retreat from relationships, forget about returning text messages, and hope that you'll give them space until they're ready to come back swinging.

## PLAYING WELL WITH OTHERS: RELATING TO AN EIGHT WHEN YOU AREN'T ONE

Is there an Eight who has been alternately making your entire life and driving you nuts at the same time? Here's your chance to learn how to love them better and confront them appropriately when you feel them taking over too much. Additionally, we have a lot to learn from Eights about taking up more space, refusing to wait for permission to live our truest lives, and just generally giving fewer fucks. Life is too short to give a fuck about everything, boo. Try mimicking that Eight and relinquish the need to please people at the expense of your wholeness.

Now, dating an Eight is bound to be a little infuriating from time to time. That is kinda their charm. Fighting is flirting for an

Eight—they want to spark with you and see what you're made of. Can you keep up? Because most folks can't. If you can hold your own against an Eight while not dismissing them, that's the sweet spot, honey. Hold on to that.

The most important thing Eights teach us is that nobody is going to give us permission to live our truth, and if we wait on that, we'll be waiting forever. Our joy is our responsibility, and ours alone.

## DRAGON HUDDLE

All right, baby Eights, gather round. Let's have a chat.

Your vulnerability is the greatest gift you can give to the people you love. Don't just sell tickets to the You show. Keep your shit protected as much as you need to, but recall that to be loved you have to let someone in. It will not feel safe to be seen. My friends like to refer to vulnerability as "brain nudes," which is a great way of describing the involved choice that revealing your truth to someone requires. Don't trust everyone, but trust someone. I promise that, regardless of the outcome, taking the opportunity to show up as yourself is never a thing to regret it, even if the person you showed up for ends up being trash. That skill will follow you into any relationship.

You are so much, and the world needs every ounce of you. Those who shrink away from your fullness are not your people. Avoidance is a fucking drug. Let them live their smaller lives. Look for the people who can meet you, who can approach your energy without fear, look it in the eyes, and respond accordingly. Real recognizes real, you feel me?!

Remember that your intuition is housed in your body, and only when you are in a right relationship with him or her or them can you access its full potential. Approach that relationship with all the gentleness and nurturance of your Two integration—it requires your presence and your patience.

Now is the time to fully revel in your lust for life. You are vibrant, effortlessly alert, and alive, and we desperately need your leadership, your power, and your generosity. Eights are the people who can run countries or companies or churches, and at their healthiest, they know when to challenge and when to shut up. Cultivate that intuition slowly, and be patient with the time it takes to get your whole self into focus. You've got this. You've got anything you set your mind to, so set it to gentleness and generosity. There is no one more capable to grow into those spaces than you.

As my friend Stacey says, "Detonate wisely, friends."

I'M A
MILLENNEAGRAM
EIGHT, SO

**NICE TRY,
BITCH.**

# MILLENNEAGRAM
# 9

## THE WALLFLOWER

"

The most precious gift we can offer
others is our presence.
When our mindfulness embraces those
we love, they will bloom like flowers.

**THICH NHAT HANH,**
*LIVING BUDDHA, LIVING CHRIST*

I WAS A TRAIN WRECK WHEN I MET HIM, STRUNG OUT AND fed up and at the end of my rope physically, emotionally, and artistically. I first heard his voice on the radio, coming through my car speakers every Thursday morning at precisely 7 a.m., a dependable ray of sunshine in the middle of my week. I tweeted something about how much that one little half hour mattered to me—how much it stood out as a breath of fresh air in my otherwise chaotic life—and before long, he slid into those DMs and I was seeing him every day.

Spending time with Joel was almost frustratingly peaceful. I often felt like I needed to add a little drama, a little intrigue to our routine. We would do one of four things every time I saw him: take a walk through the park, drink iced coffee, go eat Mexican food, or watch a movie and fall asleep next to each other. *How could he possibly be satisfied with this little life?* I wondered. And yet every morning, I found myself ready to face the day in front of me—like a weight had been lifted from my shoulders and I could breathe again. That shit was all him.

*Is this what rest feels like?* I'd think as I drove home, sipping the cold brew he'd prepared the night before for me to take to work. It was like I could hear my own heartbeat again, like I could see the world around me instead of hurrying past it. My rhythm was slower and my breathing calmer. Joel was my daily reset button.

Most folks like to call this number the peacemaker, and while I get it, it's kind of a misnomer. Yes, Nines are the kind of people who could comfortably maintain things the way they are forever, but the fact is, being a peacemaker would require venturing onto the plane of conflict, and your average Nine is not about that life, honey. I like to call them Wallflowers, because they're probably gonna sit this one out.

Like your friendly neighborhood stoner, a Nine is usually calm, dependable, passive, and immovable. While everybody else is all over the place with their feelings, a Nine prefers to maintain, to stay the course. They work hard, but their timeline is at least a couple of years longer than the rest of ours. They will stay at a job they don't care about, keep plodding away in a stagnant relationship, and persevere in less-than-ideal circumstances longer than most of us would dream of. A Nine doesn't automatically assume that change is inherently better than what's in front of them.

Enneagram queen Suzanne Stabile says that Nines "start off slow and then taper off," and, like, truer words?! My Nine friend Anna once said that her emotional landscape was like "the lazy river at a water park." If all your friends are TV shows, Nines are *Downton Abbey*. Nah, still too many poisonings and car wrecks. Nines would be Bob Ross's *The Joy of Painting*! They're not doing anything real big, but they're doing it real nice, and people are soothed by having their stable, settled presence up in their space. It's nigh-on impossible to hate Nines, if only because they literally wouldn't dream of pulling some shit that you could even remotely find offensive or off-putting. They get offended by other folks' offensiveness. Yeah, I know. There are layers here.

Now, what I don't mean is that Nines don't get angry or aren't secretly digging an emotional pit of abrasive opinions—hell, you've never met a human more overcome with resentful, eviscerating thoughts that rarely see the light of day. I have a theory that it's the bottling them up that makes them meaner. But peacekeeping requires bottling.

## THE CONS OF BEING A WALLFLOWER

I call Nines the Wallflowers not because they're insecure, introverted, and just waiting to get asked to dance. Nines are active, engaging individuals. While they get a bad rap for being "lazy," they're rarely actually lazy. Nines, however, are often wallflowers to their own lives. Suspicious of grand gestures and glacial when it comes to making decisions, Nines allow themselves to be pulled into the stream of life and carried down it with no resistance.

Not all middle kids are Nines, but are all Nines middle kids? These unassuming cuties have a lot in common with stereotypical middle children. Feeling neglected or overlooked is often a thorn in the side of your fave Nine. They grew up under the misconception that whatever shit they wanted or had to say was not valued on the same level as those around them, so they became both quiet and resentful.

Perhaps in their family safety meant shrinking. Perhaps they were legitimately overlooked and deemed less interesting than their dramatic siblings. At some point, the message was lost that their voice mattered, that their childhood feelings were valid, and their concerns and complaints were not heard. This lens then colored all future relationships—and it's an insidious motherfucker, because the whole point of this particular lens is that it makes the Nine unassuming. Almost invisible. We are all essentially still the same small, scared kid souls whose corresponding bodies we left behind in puberty. Our Nine just decided back then they had to stop needing things and often take over their own care from their dismissive, disengaged, or just downright too-busy parents (and no shade to parents, honestly, because they are also human, and humans fuck up—it's literally our MO).

In order to preemptively manage what they already expect to be the case, Nines tend to engage in self-erasure, minimizing or outright scrubbing their own experiences from the annals of life. It takes an extra sort of self-awareness for a Nine to come to terms with the fact that they've been repressing their memories and emotions, content to be affable wallflowers on the dance floor of life. Again—and

I will drive this home till y'all get it—Nines eat repressed resentment for breakfast, and just because they're not aware of it doesn't mean it's not there, lurking beneath the surface of interactions. A dialed-in friend can occasionally pick up on the tension a Nine feels, expending all their emotional energy on suppressing the feelings causing their discomfort. Unfortunately, a good fucking bit of the time discomfort and truth go hand in hand—those bitches. Am I right?!

The growth edge here is for a Nine to reclaim their power from whomever the fuck they've passively given it to, or at least haven't demanded it back from. What may feel like selfishness to a Nine may just be autonomy, after all.

## PASSION: APATHY

Nines prefer not to worry much about dramatic shit like dreams and desires, so their particular passion is best described as apathy. Some people call it laziness, but given the fact that Nines are almost always busy as fuck helping other people, managing their home, and maintaining their emotional equilibrium (which in and of itself is a lot of work, to be honest), "laziness" is the wrong word.

What Nines lack is insight into their true selves, an ability to differentiate between themselves and the people around them. It's almost as if, in recognizing the Big Feelings and Big Needs of others, they decide their own can wait. They're in no rush, which is cool, but when they prioritize other folks long enough, they end up never getting around to themselves. Nines tend to blend into the plans and passions of their partners and closest friends, making the boundaries of their true selves rather vague and difficult to make out. In a friend group, everybody likes the Nines, but who are they, exactly?

All too often they don't know themselves.

## SURVIVAL STORY: SELF-FORGETTING

There's a scene in the new queer canon film *Call Me By Your Name* where Elio is reading the cute older dude he prolly shouldn't be hitting on some pensive piece of literature and there is a coded question in the excerpt that he reads aloud, his poolside lounging languid, his question urgent. (Long live Timotheé Chalamet, the light of my life and the apple of my eye.) He repeats the question, until grad school boy-man hears the longing behind his voice.

*"Will you speak or will you die?"*

Each of us came to a crossroads of sorts at some point, a moment when we chose between looking ourselves in the eye and avoiding risk. Although this is a wildly human experience, it's a microcosm of a Nine's life. Not only does a Nine struggle to speak, they also have difficulty even acknowledging their truth for fear it will upset their carefully balanced equilibrium. Life is happening all the time, and a Nine sort of wishes it wouldn't. The survival story of self-forgetting tells the Nine that true peace comes with disconnecting from the self—jumping out of the fever flow of human experience and watching it from a secluded shoreline.

But ignoring the ebbs and flows, the heights and peaks, of the human experience leaves a person with a sad and stunted sort of life. To truly enjoy, one must truly risk. A Nine confuses detachment and nonattachment, and, no bitch, those are not synonyms. (It's cool—I was confused too.)

Detachment, as author and teacher Sandra Maitri so deftly revealed in *The Enneagram of Passions and Virtues*, is its own kind of attachment—we attach to not attaching! Is someone you know afraid of commitment, of movement, of choosing one path over another at a pivotal fork in the road? The fear that keeps them in defense mode is often a fear of being affected or harmed by something or someone, and as such, that person gives an immense amount of power to the thing they seek to avoid.

Nonattachment, on the other hand, gives one the freedom to explore the breadth of the human experience, openhearted and openhanded. Nonattachment says, *I will enjoy you today, exactly as you are, remaining present, and letting you go when I must.* Presence is the key to nonattachment. It allows a person to express a spectrum of emotions—grief, joy, ecstasy, loss—without allowing the emotions to define or derail that person. Nonattachment is actually the answer to the Nine's need for equilibrium, allowing them peacefulness and presence at the same time. Talk about some fucking integration, yo!

## THE TYRANNY OF PASSIVITY

When nothing is as important as calm and balance, a lot of growth can be sacrificed.

Both Sixes and Nines experience a phenomenon I like to call "bunker brain." They both are concerned with being prepared for anything. For Sixes, it's an anxiety thing. For Nines, it's a foresight thing. In order to maintain their status quo, Nines have everything they need in the event of a crisis. They're all about that prep work. Bread and water line the walls. Emergency plans are taped up on the door in boldface print. Nines will move into their catastrophe bunkers long before a first sign of trouble, ya know, just on the off chance a freak pipe bomb lands on their lawn.

The trouble with a hypothetical, though, is that it's rarely the thing that actually happens. It's merely what could happen and, as such, has little or no bearing on reality. While Nines value caution and forethought, this emphasis can lead to catastrophizing and retreat. Because the worst *could* happen, nothing does. Because the worst is *possible*, Nines would rather not act at all.

What they fail to realize, however, is that choosing nothing is choosing something after all. And far too often the people a Nine is trying to spare by making no decisions end up being hurt by the Nine's unwillingness to act.

## WINGS

Because the Nine is such a moldable fucking number, they tend to take on the behaviors and mannerisms of their wing numbers in a big way. Their wings are Eight (the Dragon) and One (the Machine). Nines are already defensive to fears, both outside themselves and within, so their wing number tips their scale a bit one way or the other.

A 9w8 is like the eye of a fucking hurricane—outwardly calm, but you can feel that shit brewing around you. To quote the Bible, it hems you in before and behind. A more angsty iteration of the Nine energy, a 9w8 tends to struggle to make up their mind and also kinda takes offense when you do. A 9w8 picks and jabs at the people they see as inflammatory, dramatic, or overly emotional. It's rarely quite outright conflict, but one can feel a general sense of disapproval at one's choices.

A 9w1, on the other hand, displays as more anxious and perfectionistic, concerned less with whistle blowing and more with creating the perfect home space and staying there. A 9w1 isn't really a "put yourself out there" kinda bitch. They prefer to see who comes to them and then mold themselves to the specifications of that person, who is usually a more front-and-center type. Content to chill in the background and do their part, a 9w1 is particularly uninterested in drawing attention. They will adhere to a strict moral code and live a quiet, ethical, small, and happy life—that's about all a 9w1 will ask for.

## INSTINCTUAL VARIANTS

### Self-Preserving Nines

I once playfully called Joel my "comfort daddy" because this boy was quite literally the king of comfort. He was always imagining new ways to be cozy. He knew just where to put the TV in the bedroom and position his pillows for optimal ease. When I moved into a new apartment, he intuited that I would need additional airflow in my bedroom, so he bought me a box fan as a housewarming present. Self-Pres Nines are quintessential nesters. They're always putzing around the house, doing little DIY projects to make shit more comfortable. This preoccupation, however, can get in the way of accomplishing the Nine's actual plans—there's always tomorrow, ya know?

### Social Nines

Social Nines are what we think of when we call the Nines peacemakers. They're very invested in the immediate families, blood or otherwise, that surround them, and in mitigating all conflict so that peace and good humor can reign supreme. They will do everything they can to conform to the expectations of their trusted few—not so much because they actually need the affirmation, but because rocking the boat feels like a lot of emotional work. These are the folks who struggle to say no, even when everything in them is screaming to.

After years of conforming, however, a Nine may begin to feel kinda nihilistic about how their life is always the same—but it often takes years for them to come to that realization.

## Sexual Nines

Sexual Nines—more geared toward intimate, one-on-one relationships—tend to find partners who are more expressive, passionate, or even domineering than they are, and they slowly begin to morph into that person, or that person's greatest sidekick. The couple's ideas, opinions, interests, and hobbies start to look strangely similar after a few months of them being together. Merged Nines don't see the problem here—like, that's just good partnership, right?! But after a while, the whole "shadow" routine can start to wear on the person being shadowed.

## THE CHANGE CHALLENGE: INTEGRATION AND DISINTEGRATION FOR THE NINE

The more that Nines can define who they are, what they care about, and where they're going, the more they're able to head in the positive direction of the Three. This, almost more than any other integration, is a remarkable thing to behold. Passive, good-natured, just-this-side-of-lazy Nines can suddenly take on positions of leadership they wouldn't have been caught dead in before. There is an easy, balanced, inner-peace quality to this iteration of a Three—you get the sense that shit is handled and, like, in a positive, healing way.

Taking on a more active role in their workplace or community can just lay a Nine right the fuck out. I've had Nines come up and tell me that after a particularly difficult conversation or long work shift, their bodies literally involuntarily fall asleep. And yet, as the process of integration takes hold, a Nine will find they suddenly have more energy to take up space and take on leadership. I don't know much about George Washington other than what I've heard in *Hamilton* and crap homeschool history books, but I imagine he was in this kind of position. Here's a dude of not many words, who had to hire a wild young upstart to do all his correspondence, elected to be the very first president of a young and troubled nation. All this poor old war general wanted was to head home and hang out with his cherry trees (which he eventually did). And yet, when duty called, he did the best he could in a position he never wanted. Nine goes to Three. There ya go.

Nines under stress move from peaceful avoidance to almost manic activity—they disintegrate in stress to an anxious Six, almost as if everything that hasn't been tended to has to be tended to at once. The cynicism they've been trying to hide from the world and themselves rises to the surface, like maybe shit isn't actually so rosy after all. This is the point when Nines start to bring up long-held grudges or complaints they've been sitting on for fear of conflict. Might as well handle all the stress in one go, eh?! These kids are like volcanoes—just because it looks like a delightful grassy mountain doesn't mean lava hasn't been accumulating beneath it for years.

What's fortunate about disintegration for Nines is that all of this shit they've been suppressing has gotta get out in order for them to make a solid crack at personal growth. I'll say this several times through the course of this book, but our emotions—specifically anger, in this case—are stored in our bodies, just waiting for the day when we set them free. There may have to be a storm before there's calm, and that's okay.

## PLAYING WELL WITH OTHERS: RELATING TO A NINE WHEN YOU AREN'T ONE

If you're close to a Nine—a friend, partner, family member   you're probably already aware that they're hard to connect to. It's a symptom of their whole good-natured vagueness. You might spend every day with a Nine and get into a cozy little rhythm, then realize that you're not actually learning anything new about them.

Remember Joel, the Nine boyfriend I introduced you to? As adorable as our little four-activity routine was, I realized about three months in that I knew exactly the same amount of facts about this man as I had when our domestic cycle began. It was jarring to realize that our intimate arrangement hadn't actually brought us closer at all! I ran back through our experiences, trying to pinpoint times when I had provided him with new information about myself and vice versa. While I had been forthcoming (no surprise here) almost

**45**

to the point of exhibitionism, he had laughed, nodded, made me laugh, and withheld.

On the flip side, however, a Nine who has chosen to get close to somebody (which takes some doing, as you can imagine) has the propensity to merge with their loved one, taking on their interests, mannerisms, and even social and political beliefs as if they had always been the same. Being someone's clone is not sexy, y'all! Nines are susceptible to being molded, whether consciously or unconsciously, to fit the specifications of demanding or aggressive partners. It can be difficult to distinguish where the other ends and the Nine begins. They take the whole "two becoming one" thing pretty fucking seriously.

The challenge for a Nine in a relationship is to remember that their partnership does not hinge on their obedience to their loved one's opinions and idiosyncrasies. They are still a whole person partnered to a whole person, both of whom have the agonizing human luxury of choosing each other daily. Commitment is an active choice, not a passive acquiescence. And as someone in a relationship with a Nine, I say it's good to encourage a Nine to find their own hobbies—their own lives—to participate in, separate from their partner.

Nines as friends are the sort of hearty folks you can weave reliably into the tapestry of your life. You can trust them to hold firm and to stand the test of time. As long as you're able to give them the space to process changes in their own time and on their own terms—as long as you can welcome them into your space precisely as they are, not ask them to be more—you're golden.

## AN INVITATION TO DANCE

My dear Nine, baby, darlin': do you know what you need?

No, I'm not telling you. I'm asking. I'm inviting you to come away from the wall, dear wallflower, and into the dance of your life.

While everything within you may be screaming otherwise, the best shit you can do for yourself is to remain in the moment. You may have a propensity for harboring grudges or have fears about the future, but the only part of your life that is guaranteed is the now part. All you have is this moment, here, as you read this line.

As a Nine, you have a variety of mechanisms that keep your presence comfortably at bay: avoidance, merging with others, self-denial, and self-forgetfulness. Your challenge is how to act in the interest of yourself without becoming selfish, to center yourself without forgetting. It's a delicate balance, but if anyone's got this, it's my baby Nines.

Are you aware of what you're not asking for? Are you familiar with the parts of yourself you've been avoiding, for fear of introducing chaos or imbalance to your life? Admitting it really is the first step—clichés are clichés for a reason. Once you're aware of your own needs—your own expansiveness—is there a chance you could voice them? Can you ask for what you need? Can you say "Yes" to this and "No" to that? Can you decipher between what you want and what you're merely accepting? Can you stand in your truth even when it makes you uncomfortable or, worse, causes someone else discomfort? Have you fallen asleep to who you were meant to be?

*Will you speak or will you die?*

A horrifying thought, I know, but worth reflecting on. You got this.

Of course this all sounds a bit dramatic.

You will most likely not die.

But will you LIVE?

Denying yourself the full spectrum of your humanity is, after all, its own little death.

This body you're in right now will live only once. All of its joys, sensations, griefs, and ecstasies will pass with you. The body is an instrument, a writing utensil, pen and ink. It's your call what you write with it, but never forget that opting out of authorship is a kind of writing too. Write. Live. Get off the wall and dance.

> I'M A
> MILLENNEAGRAM
> NINE, SO
>
> ## LET'S ALL JUST CHILL OUT, DUDE.

# MILLENNEAGRAM
# 1

## THE MACHINE

"

You only have to let the soft animal
of your body love what it loves.

MARY OLIVER, "WILD GEESE"

I PICKED UP THE PHONE, AND MY NEW FRIEND COREY WAS ON the line, practically panting from excitement. "I have news for you, Hannah!" he exclaimed. "I entered our names for that workshop we talked about teaching!"

"Oh," I responded, trying to sound stoked. "I, uh, I already submitted that."

There was a dramatic pause. I inserted some nervous laughter and followed up quickly with "But it's totally fine, man. Don't worry about it!"

"I can't BELIEVE I did that. How did I make that mistake?" he said, repeating the same line more times than I believed was humanly possible for a person to say in one conversation. He seemed truly undone that he was capable of this small, benign error. "COREY"—I was cackling now—"it's REALLY FINE, MAN!"

"I'm just gonna be kicking myself for the next hour and a half is all." He sighed. I giggled and hung up, thinking, *There's no WAY, right? Like, surely he's fine.*

Oh. Oh. There's a way.

I was ten minutes deep into a Netflix binge when the texts started coming in.

"I just kinda wanna set myself on fire right now," the first message read. Casual.

"WHAT THE FUCK, COREY. STOP," I replied, literally LOLing at my phone.

"I should be DRAWN AND QUARTERED and THEN set on fire" was the super chill and very logical response.

For the next EXACTLY one and a half hours, Corey texted me all the creative ways he could bring about his own death. Toward the end, now thoroughly appalled and recognizing him as the case study in Millenneagram One nonsense that he was, I responded, "Jesus, Corey, is this what it's like to live inside your head?"

"You have no idea" was the reply.

## TOURING THE FACTORY

We're all familiar with the ole internal critic, but to say that's the situation Ones have going on would be the understatement of the century. Many Ones report that their internal situation is more like a whole fucking courtroom, with part of them playing lawyer and advocating on their behalf, part of them playing the whole-ass skeptical jury, and another part just straight-up judging the shit out of themselves. If a One makes a mistake, they are their biggest critic.

They ask themselves, *How did I let this happen? What should I have done?* I just broke out into a cold sweat imagining existing under that kind of pressure. The gravity, earnestness, and exacting nature of the One really lends itself to judginess. I mean, they judge themselves. Okay, maybe I mean they judge others too. LOVE Y'ALL.

I've called the One the Machine not because they're in any way inhuman, but because the expectations they have of themselves often don't take their humanity into account. Expecting perfection of yourself only works if you're made of steel.

Take some classic Ones from TV: My absolute most favorite One is Chidi from *The Good Place*, an adorable ethics professor so caught up in doing the right thing that—spoiler alert—he goes to the Bad Place just because he made his friends and fam miserable with his indecision, when he couldn't figure out which was the *right* decision.

Arguably the most iconic One on television is Leslie Knope, of *Parks and Recreation*, a fervent and committed member of the Pawnee Parks and Rec Department with big dreams, an unflagging determination, and an almost obnoxious optimism. She is obvs very concerned with everything being correct all the time. She is always making binders for everything. Adorable.

Both Chidi and Leslie carry some big-ass expectations of themselves. Classic Ones. What other people often don't realize when a One is hard on them is that there is never a point at which a One is being harder on you than they are being on themselves.

Ones are principled, responsible, and often perfectionistic—careful not to do anything before making sure it's the right thing. When they're healthy, their intuitive vision allows them to see a dozen steps ahead. Unlike your typical fly-by-the-seat-of-your-pants visionary, Ones can see what needs to be done and also the exact strategic steps to take in order to reach their goal. A One is the sort of person you can trust to be dependably correct—more so than even they realize.

## PASSION: ANGER

The passion of the One is anger—even though you won't see it expressed half the time. Tamping down pesky emotional reactions like anger is a goddamn full-time job. Ones are endlessly principled about how and when they will let you see that side of them. They are prepared as fuuuuuck—you feel me? These jokers do everything 110 percent and as such are careful not to bite off more than they can chew (oh, for this gift!). Literally nothing makes me think unhealthy One like Sarah Jessica Parker's character in *The Family Stone*, all turtlenecks and high-powered phone calls and a finely whittled, delicately filigreed stick up her ass. Anger builds in a person's body when they don't release it, and it's gonna find its way out sooner or later.

The One's anger and resentment may not be as immediately apparent as the surface wrath of the Eight, but the One is an Intuitive Triad number, and, boy, does it earn its place in the gut triad with mountains of carefully suppressed emotions, just chilling in the body, taking up space! Totally healthy! Totally not a super-common cause of sexual repression and self-harm at all! Where the Eight's fear directs their energy outward and the Nine has a little bit of both inward and outward focus, the One's energy is aimed inward, toward the self, trying to temper their reactions and behavior with careful reflection before attempting shit.

Their biggest fear is being bad, wrong, or fucked up in some way—the Machine breaking down. Of course being good is a tall order, and most of us comfortably settle for doing, like, mostly good shit and hope our petty fuckery sorta evens itself out in the end. This is not good enough for a One. When they do something in a less than perfect way, they self-flagellate like a monk who's into whips, and not in the fun kinky way.

This compulsive need for correctness leads Ones to edit their lives constantly, cutting and pasting and backspacing that shit until they get it just right. They defer decision-making of any kind until they can be completely sure of their choice, even though it's a truth universally acknowledged that humans can't be sure of shit. Of course all of this hemming and hawing and anxiety gets in the way of, like, being alive.

## SURVIVAL STORY: THE LOST MESSAGE

Now that we've set the stage a bit, let's delve deep into the One's business like the nosy voyeurs we are.

Riso and Hudson report that there is a lost childhood message for every one of the numbers—something each type needed to hear as a kid but somehow didn't. I don't necessarily attribute this to a fault of parenting, but to just a need that fell through the cracks. When we're kids, we don't know what kind of affirmation we need. All we know is what we receive. As adults, our job is to re-parent ourselves with the truth, even when our deepest wish is that someone else would have told us back then what we need. We are our own parents now.

The lost message for the One child is the assertion "You are good." You are enough. Your value exists outside of your rightness. There is no vengeful deity tending your scorecard, waiting for you to fail. Your mattering does not hang in the balance.

## THE JUDGING RUT AND THE RIGHTING RUT

At a certain point, being perfect in every space becomes a really tall order, and a lot of Ones cope by living a trapdoor life—carrying on the whole perfection thing in all spaces but one, somewhere they can let their hair down, hell, maybe even wild out a bit. This measured release can help the One blow off some steam, but ultimately it isn't much in the way of a long-term fix. The only kind of real fix, Ones, is seeing yourself truthfully and unconditionally loving the person you find therein. (Yeah, I said "therein." Just . . . go with it.)

There are a couple of brain ruts that you're gonna have to face up to, One, if you hope to dig yourself up outta those tendencies inside you. I call them the Judging Rut and the Righting Rut. Caveat here: These are not actual diagnosable complexes—I don't want y'all sending your therapists after me, 'kay? Chill. I want you to see these ruts not as chronic diseases but as temporary conditions you have the power to FIX.

The Judging Rut is precisely what it sounds like: the impetus to rescue people from their shitty life choices. I know, girl. The need runs deep. You see friends getting back together with abusive exes or throwing their life savings away or driving home tipsy from bars, and you know better, and I feel your pain. You see friends believing harmful things about themselves and workplaces being run inefficiently and injustices being done. You're right about all of it, you really are. But what is the most helpful thing here? To beat people over the head with their wrongness or to be present and patient and let them learn themselves? It super blows, but honestly, that's how a lot of folks learn. Some people just have to put their precious little fingers on hot stovetops to learn how not to get burned. You may save them from a mistake today, but you will not be righting the long-term wrong. You're prolonging the inevitable, and, boo, that is not a kindness. All that does, honestly, is make you feel better about yourself. Which is selfish.

Yikes—am I right?

The second, and extremely related, brain rut is the Righting Rut. The Venn diagram of the Judging Rut and the Righting Rut are two mostly overlapping circles. I separate them because I think each has a slightly different motivation behind it. If the Judging Rut is about correcting other people (though mostly to satisfy yourself), then the Righting Rut is a general reflex toward changing all that is wrong with their own little universe and the world at large. It's like a knee-jerk reaction that turns Ones into that meme where the scrawny white kid in class is holding himself back from saying some shit to the point that he's red in the face and veins are popping right the fuck out of his neck. Y'all know the one, right? Or do I spend too much time on Twitter? Answer is probably both there. I DIGRESS.

## WINGS

Ones can have either a Nine wing (1w9) or a Two wing (1w2). 1w9s tend to be more abstract thinkers and dreamers, sorting out the big questions of society and politics and religion—that big-picture shit, you feel? They don't bother with less visible hills, partly because the Nine wing keeps them from exerting energy on what they feel are lost causes. They're all about conservation of energy, those Nines. 1w9s tend to be kinda generally disappointed by other humans, who they perceive as being pretty generally hellbent on making bad choices and fucking up their lives. However, when 1w9s choose to engage with someone, they're able to display a generosity and a compassion that makes them both dependable and life-giving friends. "Criticism, but make it therapy," reads my 1w9 Millenneagram mug, and ain't that the truth?

The more active 1w2s are the reformers and do-gooders of the One spectrum. They've never met a mess they aren't willing to dive into and fix for, ya know, the "greater good." Often more engaging and engaged than their Nine-wing counterparts, 1w2s may use more aggressive means for getting mischief managed. Leaning into a Two wing might make a One turn into a bit of a meddler, getting all up in your business, trying to persuade you to let them fix your mistake. As they travel down the levels of unhealth, 1w2s may become more vocal about their complaints and discontentedness, and find themselves more negatively affected by their surroundings than their counterparts.

## INSTINCTUAL VARIANTS

### Self-Preserving Ones

Self-Pres Ones are the most fixated on getting all their physical needs met, and they encounter a lot of internal conflict when their needs clash with their crazy-high self-expectations. My fellow former evangelicals—ex-vangelicals, as some of us like to be called—will pick up on some downright Augustine shit here. Augustine, an early Christian church father, hot and bothered by the "needs of the flesh" (LOLOLOL, let me translate: SEX) and convinced that it was a sin to act on these urges, wrote into being some truly heinous ideas about purity that were later siphoned into twentieth-century evangelicalism for all of us to be fucked up by all these centuries later. Thanks, Augustine!

Remember Chidi from *The Good Place*? He's a great example of a Self-Pres One, so overcome by the weight of making the Right Decision that he never makes any, catastrophizing worst-case scenarios much like an average Six would. (A lot of average Ones and Sixes confuse themselves for each other.)

## Social Ones

Social Ones consider themselves teachers, more invested in their communities and social circles than the other subtypes. They believe they hold the answers that will make shit better. They also like exposing errors, bringing folks to justice, and working for reform in their areas of interest and expertise. The more unhealthy they are, the more their opinions can err on the rigid side of things, and as they spiral down the levels, they tend to believe it's their way or the highway. Social Ones see themselves as examples, modeling right behavior for others to look up to and mirror. It's not strictly an image thing, though, because Social Ones genuinely want to be what it is they're projecting. They're deeply concerned about the goodness they portray being an accurate representation of what's going on inside. Sounds like A Lot.

## Sexual Ones

The intimately focused subtype, the Sexual One, is more concerned with perfecting people they are in a relationship with than themselves or society. They are deeply invested in their relationships and bring an intensity to those connections that is very gut triad. Their anger sits closer to the surface than it does with other Ones, and they are more obviously fired up about the shit they care about. These folks read as the reformers, the Martin Luthers of their time, writing 95 freaking theses about what's wrong with their partners, community, and the world, and then hammering them to the doors of their neighborhood for all to see. Gotta love a bitch with some dramatic flourish—am I right?

## BETTER THAN PERFECT: INTEGRATION AND DISINTEGRATION FOR THE ONE

So much of being a human animal with the DISEASE of consciousness is found in the gray areas of life and, as such, can feel like risky business to the One, who looks for the black and white in everything. It's hard to determine what is right or correct about undependable things like "play" or "sex" or "connection" or, lady-god forbid, "spontaneity." The One's natural tendency to shut shit down that cannot be easily categorized is beautifully counteracted by the One's integration to Seven, though. Told y'all. Good news.

A One in stability, holding on to all the earnestness and kind caution of their number, will integrate to Seven and live fully present in the here and now—not only with their friends and lovers but also with their true selves. The strength of the Seven is in its pure, unadulterated ability to enjoy the fuck out of life—to accept one's impulses, desires, and circumstances and make some fresh-ass lemonade out of whatever mixed bag that is. A One moving toward Seven will fix less and enjoy more.

An integrated One is dependable, careful, clear, thoughtful, and so goddamn earnest, y'all! It's like: GET SOME GUILE. You're a human person—Jesus. You will never have to worry about a healthy One pulling some backhanded, deceptive shit on you, which means they're expecting the same from you. They're on some scout's honor shit, okay? You've been warned. By integrating to Seven, they have the capacity to tap into their lightheartedness, to enjoy adventures and other delightfully unplanned things, and to express their gut emotions instead of repressing them.

As a member of the Intuitive Triad, integration for a One means owning their intuition—recognizing that their wisdom comes FROM their body, not in spite of it. One of the lies of Western capitalism that we all have internalized to some extent is that all dependable knowledge comes from cold, hard reason and quantifiable facts. As a culture, we have largely lost the art of listening to ourselves, and no number more so than the One.

The One integration is often not a smooth transition, so buckle up, pups. There will probs be growing pains, where the brain starts freaking the fuck out. After white-knuckling it through years of repression, organization, and strict adherence to standards, that pent-up One energy doesn't exactly go quietly into the night. May I suggest screaming off of cliffs occasionally? Just spitballing here.

On the flip side, though, an unhealthy One is a terrifying thing to behold. Ones go to Four in unhealth, which means they internalize all the outsider complex and "nobody gets it" nature of the Four while still espousing their unmeetable expectations. This spiral sends them hurtling away from relationships and connection and into self-pity territory, which is a horrible murky place that sucks them into the ground like a damn *NeverEnding Story*–level swamp.

## PLAYING WELL WITH OTHERS: RELATING TO A ONE WHEN YOU AREN'T ONE

If you're tryna be in a relationship with a One, it's important to understand that these motherfuckers like their shit real sorted. Nothing gray or done halfway will do, so if you plan on fucking with a One, lemme offer you this sage piece of advice: don't. If you want to feel the full retributive action of a wounded gut-triad number, then be my guest, but don't come crying to me when it blows up in your face.

One of the best things you can do for a One is to graciously let them know when their standards are too high for you, or for themselves. They just want to be the perfect partner, friend, son, whatever, but a lot of times they need their shoulders gently shaken to get them off the perfection spiral and back into the glorious frustration that is real life. Remind them there are billions of different right ways to be, and that what works for them may not work for you, and that's okay. Remind them they are the perfect partner, friend, son for YOU, and you love them, warts and all.

Also, remember that Ones are not robots, 'kay? They're people too—just the kind that will probably make fewer mistakes than you in the course of your relationship. Obnoxious, I know, but let's just let them have this one. They prolly care about it more than you do—let's be real. Remember that your One is a human person with a big ole earnest heart, a sense of humor, and a need to be reminded that they're better than perfect: they're GOOD.

## TUNING UP TOGETHER

Recognize, my dear sweet baby Ones, that every hill is not a hill you gotta die on. I know it feels like it sometimes. I know compromises can feel like slippery slopes. I know it seems stupid to not correct what is to YOU an obvious problem. The problems are many and they are everywhere: in your workplace, in your family, in your home, and in yourself. A huge growth edge for you will be to realize that just because something is best for you, that doesn't mean it's best for someone else. WILD, I know. And if the problem you find is one that's in yourself, the best way to fix it is not by shaming yourself for having it. The only thing shame does is exacerbate a soul problem, like squeezing lemon juice into an open wound. It hurts like hell and does literally nothing useful.

Breathe through the panic that comes when the Judging Rut or the Righting Rut show up on your path, and practice actively walking around them. Your brain likes its cute little patterns—those specific pathways are programmed into it—so it will keep spouting out the same shit and won't take too kindly to the new path you're charting. For better or worse, you're reliable that way.

Stick with it. Coming home to yourself takes a minute.

It's often been said that perfect is the enemy of good, and no-where does this apply more than with Ones. I know you're always challenging yourself to be a perfect partner, perfect employee, and perfect friend. It can be difficult sometimes for a One to imagine a world in which a good deal of life can't be neatly shoved into "right" and "wrong" boxes. You want to program the right answers into your brain so the right responses, the right words, the right reactions, come out.

Here's a question to ask yourself: *Do I want to be right or do I want to be happy?*

Oof. That one'll tune up those rusty joints right quick.

I hate to break it to ya, darlin', but you will not ALWAYS be able to have it both ways. There will be times when, to stay in a relationship, you'll have to navigate accepting your own wrongness, or—let's be honest—more often the wrongness of your partner. No one is telling you not to have standards, but I'm saying that humans will not always meet them. Sucks, I know.

Ones, at their essence, have the power of vision—the power to see five steps ahead, to fix broken machinery, to set things on the right course, and to see life as it should be. Coupled with compassion and empathy, freed from the bondage of both the Judging Rut and the Righting Rut, this power is transformative. One might even say redemptive, if one was in the habit of using churchy words like that. There is a right way for things to be, and that way may not be perfect, but it can be good. You challenge us, Ones, to believe that we can be good, but only after you believe it about yourself.

At your essence, Ones, you are a miracle of intuition and discernment. You are able to follow the arc of justice as it bends while the rest of us are often lost in the weeds of our own egos and emotional landscapes. Lead us, but do it gently. Grant us the grace that you have learned to grant yourself. Your goodness is not affected by your very human shortcomings, and your brokenness is not final. You are mending yourself every day,

slowly,

patiently,

inch by loving inch.

# HOW EACH TYPE FUCKS UP THEIR LOVE LIFE

## Ones

I mean, I can work with *this* I guess. You've got . . . potential. (YOU'RE NOT THEIR REAL MOM. PISS OFF.)

## Fours

I ALWAYS KNEW YOU WOULD NEVER GET ME. YOU'RE NOT DEEP ENOUGH. AND YOU DIDN'T EVEN READ THAT BOOK I CASUALLY MENTIONED BEING MY FAVORITE IN HOPES YOU WOULD CARE ENOUGH TO PORE OVER IT AND TAKE NOTES.

## Sevens

I can't help that THEY were texting ME long hours into the night about their deepest, darkest secrets. I'M ADDICTED TO CONNECTION.

## Twos

Why am I the only one who ever gives anything to this relationship??

## Threes

Hmmm. I wonder if I can date my way into X profession or social circle.

## Fives

Hello, I must retreat into my mind palace and emotionally ignore you for several major life crises. Catch you on the flip.

## Sixes

I will now commence pushing you away at different intervals and varying intensities in order to be sure you will ALWAYS COME BACK TO ME.

## Eights

MUST. MAINTAIN. CONTROL. OF THIS. AND ALL. SITUATIONS.

## Nines

Hello. I am HIGH MAINTENANCE about being LOW MAINTENANCE! If I have to believe this lie about me, SO DO YOU.

# THE
# FEELING
# TRIAD

# PART II

# HEART TYPES

## THE FEELING TRIAD

### TYPES 2, 3, AND 4

We seldom dare to be fully in our hearts.

—DON RICHARD RISO AND RUSS HUDSON,
*THE WISDOM OF THE ENNEAGRAM*

AND SO WE ARRIVE AT . . . THE DRAMA QUEENS.

Y'all know who you are.

Whattup—Feeling Triad? We out here!!!

The Feeling Triad is made up of three types—Two, Three, and

Four—that share a common gift: emotional intelligence. They're the heart. Like all human things, their emotional intelligence is both a gift AND a curse, and the Feeling Triad numbers make damn sure to use it both ways.

Being in the Feeling Triad means that a lot of the time what matters, if these types are razor-sharp honest, is the look of a thing rather than the actual truth of a thing. Heart types are the kings and queens and the nonbinary royalty of "Fake it till you make it," which is a nice cute little principle for some, but they def take it too far. They have this idea that if they see the person they want to be reflected in someone's perception of them, well, that's close enough, right? Even Fours, who build their image around being authentic, need to be seen as authentic to believe it about themselves.

It's not because they're trying to pull one over on you—they're trying to pull one over on themselves.

The Feeling types play a part—a good bit of which is kinda true. The images they project are never whole falsehoods. They may not even be half falsehoods. They're just themselves spruced up. Folks would call that "putting your best foot forward." Now, just imagine pulling that shit for the rest of your life to everybody, including yourself. I need a fucking nap.

The more powerful their feelings are, the more they try to find substitutes for those feelings. Powerful feelings scare them a bit, so they redirect their emotional energy into image creation and management. It's not comfortable to be always burning.

## DAMMING OUR RIVERS

My friend Ally was an army brat who wept over every home she left. When she was six, she was convinced that if she could just *feel* hard enough about her last home, pray hard enough for it, that somehow she would be able to go back. At night she would lie awake, sobbing silently for the ducks that had lived in the lake-backyard of their trailer on the West Coast or the super-climbable fig tree in the backyard of the first childhood home she could remember. (I hope this is all registering as pathetic.)

One night, she crept into her mom and dad's room and tapped her mom's shoulder, raising the volume on the tears juuuuust enough to be audible but not quite obnoxious. It's an art, guys.

"MoooOom," she whispered, letting her voice tremble *just* a hair more than it already was, "I need to go back and see the ducks. Please, can we just go home?"

The voice that replied was viscerally Over It.

"Ally, honey, get back in bed. You need to give this up. We're not going back, okay? I don't want to hear you cry anymore about it."

This moment registered for Ally as a turning point: she internalized the message that her wants and, more important, her feelings were not valued and had to be both squashed and handled. Ally retreated deeper into herself, creating her own imaginary emotional universe where the things she felt were felt instead by histrionic princesses, who were *allowed* to be loud and moody and anguished.

This isn't to say that Ally never expressed her emotions to her mother again. But when she did, it was with an air of defensiveness, as if to say, "You can't make me NOT feel this way." The shame she registered about feeling the "wrong" way about things caused her to hide, to act out, and to present, as often as she could, an alternative self, made in the image of her mother's desire. Mommy issues are real, y'all. This isn't unique to Fours like Ally. This is common to Twos and Threes too. Feeling types create images of themselves that either they think the people around them want to see or they themselves want to see.

I'm gonna say this a lot and you're gonna get sick of hearing it, but one of the keys to wielding the Enneagram sword in integration battle is learning how to re-parent yourself. You gotta start over with yourself—no, you *get* to start over with yourself—because in a lot of ways you're still that same lost little kid inside, trying to make sense of the world, but now you have to fake it like you know what's up. Like you know what you're doing. Fuck adulting—am I right?

There's no one right way to re-parent, y'all. Hear me on that. There's no one-size-fits-all curriculum out there that'll do the trick. You gotta write your own curriculum, a key component of penning your new survival story. Truth is, we don't all need to hear the same things. The attention and affirmation you didn't receive as a kid is reflected in your Millenneagram type, and only you can decide what you need to hear and how to comfort, soothe, and strengthen yourself.

## PERSONALITY AS A (BANGIN') STOREFRONT

As kids, the Feeling Triad, or heart types, got real fixated on the idea of identity: *Who am I? Where do I fit? How do I matter?* Everyone's true self pokes its head out pretty early on, to see if the coast is clear and if it's welcome. Kids will hit you out of nowhere with some profound shit, because the border wall between who they are and who they allow themselves to be hasn't been built yet. They live in this wild, emotional Narnia, just chilling in their own personal witchy wardrobes and deigning to grace us with their magical presence eeeevery now and again. Not to go full C. S. Lewis on you, but as a heart type myself, I often wonder whether the playground of the imagination is our truest space after all. Wow, y'all gotta reel me back here. As I was saying!

Somewhere down the line the heart types received the message that who they were—their truest selves—was not entirely welcome. That they were not enough, or perhaps were just the wrong side of too much. Riso and Hudson call this "narcissistic wounding."[1] When heart types find out they cannot fully belong in their little world, they spin a new presentation, a veneer, a storefront that will render them acceptable, useful, and valued in their home, their family, their

---

1. Don Richard Riso and Russ Hudson, *The Wisdom of the Enneagram* (New York: Bantam, 1999).

school, and their space, and this difficulty with authenticity follows them into adulthood.

Of course the pretty little storefront is hardly a full lie. It's a half-truth, at worst. It advertises what can be found inside, with rich colors and pictures and trendy typography. It beckons to shoppers—because heart types start to believe their relationships are actually transactions and love is an exchange of goods.

Channeling their emotional intelligence outward, heart types find ways to reel you in with just the right image to make them feel loved, and as a replacement for loving themselves.

Heart types are renowned for being all feelingsy, and what I'll say is that they have the CAPACITY to be. They were probably pretty feelingsy kids. I mean, you could probs rename the Feeling Triad the Tantrum Triad and not be tooooo far off from the truth. These kids were EXTRA as hell, which I'm allowed to say because I was one. The more unhealthy the Twos, Threes, and Fours are, the more they channel their emotional intelligence toward making YOU feel the right things about THEM.

If you fail to buy what they're selling, a heart type reads that as a rejection of them, when all it is ACTUALLY is you passing up on their storefront. They respond with hostility and defensiveness when their bullshit is not validated, because they carefully con-structed this identity as a placeholder for their true self, which they're worried may not actually exist anymore—that maybe their true self was never real. After selling this idealized image for long enough, they start to buy their own bullshit. But it doesn't have to be that way.

## HOW TWOS FIT INTO THE FEELING TRIAD

Each of the three Feeling Triad types constructs a different kind of storefront. The Two storefront often looks like an unassuming nonprofit or a twenty-four-hour shelter, promising gifts and labor and services if you'll only come inside. There's no catch, other than you needing them. As long as they feel that you do, and of course you clearly communicate that in some way or other, they're good to go. They can keep that good-cop routine going all goddamn day and night. They consider themselves rescuers, placed on this earth to be the helpmate you never knew you always needed.

An unhealthy Two always finds a way to take up their time with other people's needs, after which they can shout "Woe is me" from the rooftops about all the time they don't have. Their personality values both being helpful and being perceived as such. A healthy Two, on the other hand, understands where the boundaries are and joyfully offers love and support to a carefully selected few based on those boundaries. Both versions are helpers, but one is giving from a place of scarcity and the other, from abundance.

**79**

## HOW THREES FIT INTO THE FEELING TRIAD

Threes want you to like them but also want to like themselves, and this double-duty storefront action makes Threes unstoppable in pretty much any sphere of life and work they wanna break into. An unhealthy Three makes a hella good social climber. They're on some Reese Witherspoon *Vanity Fair* bullshit, yo. They're the smooth-talking, baby-kissing politician. They're strategic and re-sourceful, intuiting what needs to be said and when and just gen-erally winning at life. Of course, there's an underlying pressure for Threes to continually be winning, to be earning love and connec-tion and success, to always be doing and rarely just being, let alone feeling. They consider themselves free from rescuing, that they do not need you or your assistance, and they will waste no time proving that shit to you.

A healthy Three, though, is a real-ass game changer. Still charming and strategic, a healthy Three knows that to be loved is to be seen, and carefully, selectively, they will allow themselves to be.

## HOW FOURS FIT INTO THE FEELING TRIAD

Fours construct their storefront primarily for their own benefit—in fact, they might make it super moody and dark and abandoned look-ing so you won't want to come near it. To save themselves the pain of rejection, they go ahead and recuse themselves from whatever they see as the norm or the status quo. To save themselves the pain of not being understood, they declare everyone too basic to get them in the first place. Being "unique" is their pride and joy, their supposed "cross" to bear, and also the key to their storefront. Since they feel something about them is not right or acceptable—something that renders them an outsider—they go ahead and own that as a coping mechanism to the wound of not belonging. They see themselves as in need of saving from the world and from themselves, and if they make themselves compelling enough, maybe you'll rescue them.

Unhealthy Fours often construct their image as the antithesis to what everyone else is doing, in a super over-the-top and obvious sort of way. (Don't tell them I said that—they freaking hate being obvious.) Is everybody in their family an athlete? Well, guess what? The Four is gonna be a moody hippie art baby. Is everybody religious? Meet the new humanist! Reactive, histrionic behavior is often what passes for vulnerability with our little tortured-artist types. Healthy Fours, however, learn to catalyze their latent creativity into action and see themselves as they truly are, warts and all.

## BEING YOUR OWN DANCE DAD

At the root of the heart types' image building is a deep and abiding fear that if people really saw them for who they are, for their truest

81

selves, people would not love them; that the only way they can earn the attention and affirmation they so desperately seek is to carefully weave a web of little white lies to trap others into giving a shit.

You need attention, heart type. You need to be seen. I get it, girl. It's okay. Don't let people say "attention seeking" at you like it's some kinda insult. I mean, somebody gotta be looked at, right? But being seen just as the image you present to the world will not serve you in the long run. That shit won't stick. You have to offer yourself the attention you need. Be your own dance dad. Cheer yourself on. Whoop loudly from your own audience. Be extra in the celebration of you.

As things stand currently, if you're unhealthy or even just average, there's no chance anybody else out there has a solid handle on who the real you is, outside the cage of personality you've confined yourself to. In the words of the legendary drag queen RuPaul, "If you can't love yourself, how in the hell you gonna love somebody else?"[2]

The magic of the Enneagram is that while building veneers is your coping mechanism, being seen and known for who you really are is your actual strength. Our survival stories are often the passwords to our healing. The opposite of your brain rut holds your true strength.

2. RuPaul, Twitter feed, June 12, 2017, 9:46 a.m., https://twitter.com/rupaul/status/874306994626109440?lang=en.

Learn to think of personality as a role you play, not who you are. It is you, but only one small facet of your essence. You're bright and brilliant and multifaceted and changeable. Your true self cannot be contained by any number. You do your best to keep that self under wraps, and yet there you are, smoldering below the surface, threatening to erupt someday. And erupt you must. I'm here to tell you that you get to pick how.

The first order of business is directing all that energy you're wasting on pleasing other people toward pleasing yourself and meeting your own needs. (Somewhere out there is a Two having a heart attack right now.) Everyone's a little selfish, so don't pretend like you're not. (Okay, Twos, deep breaths.) When it comes to heart types, being selfish is key: it takes the onus off other people to validate you and heaps all that fucking responsibility back on you. After all, you cannot earn the love you need.

The gift you bring to all the numbers is emotional understanding. You see motherfuckers in their soul space, and I swear to God, that freaks people out from time to time. Don't cut back on the intensity, though. As much as you want to be seen for who you really are, you have the ability to see others for who they really are too, on a level they can't even imagine yet. You can affirm, incite, and inspire us to live into our heart spaces.

Imma let y'all in on a little secret. The magic behind integration, for every fucking one of the numbers on the Enneagram, is as simple as this: see your truth as it really is and then choose it. Cheryl

Strayed, every millennial's poet mom, says: "Whatever happens to you belongs to you. Make it yours. Feed it to yourself even if it feels impossible to swallow. Let it nurture you, because it will."[3]

Presence is just admitting what is already there. Sounds easy, but it's actually pretty fucking hard. You will never succeed at being someone else. Give up right now. You're literally wasting your breath, and you don't even know how much more of it you've got! What a bad plan, dude! Don't settle for the shell of something you wish you were. Be you, loudly and badly and gloriously. Anything else would be a lie.

You are the point of you. The truth of your deepest self, the part that still lives in the caves of your psyche, is waiting for your personality to let up and let it out. Being that person is why you're here. You have nothing to accomplish, nothing to project, other than her. Know her. Share him. Whoever they are, bear witness to them. You are the only person who can see your true self in all her glorious and terrifying entirety.

All right, now that I've good and scared y'all, let's get into it.

3. Cheryl Strayed, *Tiny Beautiful Things: Advice on Love and Life from Dear Sugar* (New York: Vintage, 2012), 133.

# MILLENNEAGRAM
# 2

## THE PARENT

"

Maybe one day I will get around to
fixing myself too.

**SLEEPING AT LAST (RYAN O'NEAL),**
**"TWO"**

WHEN I WAS A POOR, BROKE SEMINARY STUDENT AT MOODY Bible Institute in Chicago (long before I became the brazen, heathen hussy I am today), my friend Emily would take pity on me every once in a while and drag me home for a three-day weekend and home-cooked meals. One weekend, as we rode the train to southern Illinois, she raved about her mother's cooking but hardly prepared me for what I was about to encounter.

When we walked into her house, a blur of a woman bounded up to us, hugged us vigorously, and took things out of our hands at an alarming rate. When my eyes finally settled on the tornado human in front of me, it became obvious that this very small, very energetic woman was Emily's mom, and she was both entirely at my service and consummately in charge. I felt lowkey welcomed and overwhelmed at the same time, like there was instant pressure to feel comfortable as quickly as possible.

Once Emily's mom had us stripped of our possessions, hurried us into seats, and accosted us with piles of food, we became the show. She wanted to hear all about us and right away: what we were doing for work, who we were dating, and, ya know, our deepest hopes and dreams. Supes casual. As soon as she asked a question, though, there was no time to sit around and wait for a thoughtful answer, because everything was an immediate crisis that only she could solve: the teenage boy's bedroom or the preteen tiff in the family room or the casserole that needed five more minutes to brown. She was like a reverse tornado, sweeping through every room and magically sorting everything while leaving everybody in the room feeling a bit . . . dizzy. Classic Two. A dizzyingly helpful tornado.

## THE "COOL" PARENTS

You don't have to be an actual parent to be a parent—you feel me? Every group of friends has a mom, and that mom is usually a Two. Scrappy and strategic, Twos appoint themselves as the parent of whatever group they find themselves in and get to work fixing the fuck out of their appointed offspring. Twos are natural givers and helpers, the sort of folks who like to go where they fit in and become indispensable there. Because they're good at discerning wants, sometimes even before the wanter is aware of them, they're able to quickly become needed—and being needed is what Twos crave more than anything. In no time at all, and seemingly with little effort, they're an integral part of the family, a team player, a reliable sidekick, or a trusted confidante. The play is to align themselves with people doing the things they care about, and then they figure out what those people need. These kids put the "best" in best friend.

The concept of self-care is often lost on Twos, because they're so busy caring for the people around them that they forget to leave time for themselves. They're active, focused, intentional, and often intense. Twos are often a veritable microcosm of activity, whether in the workplace or at home, sorting everything out, filling in gaps, and just generally being the motherfucking MVP. Who's the GOAT? The Two's the GOAT, no question.

Chances are, if you're starting this chapter all like, *Yeah, I'm such a Two*, you're probs not, boo. Hate to burst your bubble. Fact is that all the pros of the Two type are the qualities women are taught to cultivate and embody from birth: helpfulness, attentiveness, self-sacrifice, and self-effacement. Real Twos know what the cons are, and you don't.

Twos know that being so helpful, so accessible, and so aware of others' needs is the only way to be wanted. It's not usually as explicit as all that, but Twos endeavor to earn the affection of those around them, which rarely includes asking for the things they need.

Like with actual moms, half the time the "help" Twos offer isn't even shit anyone was asking for. They shove more food onto your plate or bring you coffee even though you've already been through the Starbucks drive-thru that day, and they insert themselves into all your arguments to defend you with a passion that feels, at times, *extra*. You feel like you have to be grateful, of course, because here's somebody being a whole-ass savior, so you mutter some thanks or accept the help, and in turn, the Two gets to feel like they earned today's love—and you won't forget it because there's no chance they'll let you. You may get the sense that the Two's scorecard is always in hand, and at the first hint of ungratefulness on your part, they'll innocently remind you that the score is Them 1,000, You 3. So really you have no ground to stand on.

If only relationships were that simple—am I right?

## PASSION: PRIDE

The passion that Twos are connected with is just good old-fashioned pride—the kind that sounds like humility but doesn't really look the part. Fake humbleness. Because Twos are really concerned with keeping up the appearance of being giving and self-sacrificing, anybody coming up with a different read on their situation is immediately rendered invalid. In time, Twos may begin to wonder if they have any value or real self outside the services and labor they provide others. If that's taken away from them, what could possibly be left?

## SURVIVAL STORY: GIVE TO GET

If you were to map the relationship of each Feeling Triad number with their self-image, their status would say, "It's complicated." Twos tend to see themselves, their worth, and their impact entirely through the eyes of those around them. They very rarely look at themselves directly, for fear of encountering needs they either can't meet or don't feel permission to have. The message they internalized as kids is that they have to take care of others in order to be taken care of themselves. When they were kids, in order to receive, they had to give first. Maybe a parent relied on them too heavily. Maybe they just didn't feel seen unless they were doing the MOST. The posture of the Two is always outward and away from themselves.

This doesn't mean they're not thinking about themselves—it just means they don't feel they can afford to look like it. Here's where things start getting a tad on the shady side, when Twos start fixing other people to vicariously fix themselves or to receive the help they need as a return on their investment in others.

Unfortunately, this transactional approach to relationships undermines the connections the Two is trying to create! You shouldn't rely on passive aggression to get what you need out of life. Any relationship that requires that of you isn't one you deserve. The transaction stops being about the helping and starts being more about the reward for the helping. Strings get attached. You boutta make your partner start dancing, yo.

## THE TWO'S COMPLEXES

I feel the need to insert the professional caveat yet again here that I'm not a therapist, and consequently, me calling the following coping mechanisms "complexes" is more a shorthand term than anything else. I'm not diagnosing anyone. I'm just trying to explain fixations that may be occurring in language you can connect with. Please only let medical professionals assign mental illnesses to you, okay? There's enough of us WebMD bingeing quacks out here.

### Martyr

A Two with a martyr complex thinks that in order to be capital *G* Good they have to deny themselves their wants and wishes and just spend themselves in service of other people or the divine or who-the-fuck-ever. We see this mindset crop up a ton in Christianity, but it has permeated the socialization of young women of all religious persuasions. To be Good you have to be Unhappy. To be Whole you have to make yourself Empty. Deny thyself.

### Savior

The savior complex locks in real cozily with the martyr complex. It tells Twos (and other numbers, okay, but let's stay focused) that not only do they have to give up what they want, they also have to give others what *they* want. This mentality ensures that Twos go chasing after humans—usually men, but you know—who are miserable and sad and seemingly unable to help themselves. *I'll be the one to get through to this, dude*, Twos think. Twos often don't realize that this instinct, while rooted in kindness and empathy, magnetically draws brainless asshats attracted to these walking emotional-labor fountains like moths to a flame. All right, my metaphors broke down a bit here, but you get it.

Of course Twos feel overwhelmed and overworked when they're busy trying to save the whole world while denying themselves. I mean I'm exhausted just reading this shit.

## THE AFFECTION PROBLEM

Twos of the world, ask yourselves: Are you offering help that is needed?

No, think about it. I know you help at all times and, whenever conceivably possible, you go above and beyond. But who is your help for? Is it really for the person you're offering it to or is it serving you instead? Twos fall into the very human trap of needing to be needed when they allocate all their time and attention to others. (I can't not start singing Cheap Trick's "I waaaant you to want me" here.) Your relationship can become more about seeing yourself as a helper rather than about the actual helping.

The harsh truth of it is this: It's not enough to do nice things. It's not enough to have good intentions. (This, by the way, is also a really good rule of thumb to remember when you're wondering, *Hey, am I using my white or straight privilege right now?*) Your intentions mean shit if they're not in the best interest of the person you're directing them at. Of course, in order to figure out what is in their best interest, a lotta times ya just gotta listen. Which means less doing. Which means less recognition.

Stings a bit, don't it?

You're probably always going to have something of the parent about you, and that's good. You're you. Never hear me say to change; only hear me say to redirect. So if you're gonna be the mom of the group, decide what kind of mom that is. Which kind do you wish you'd had? Which kind would best serve your friends? In nine out of ten cases, the listening-more-and-fixing-less parent is the one that's needed, and you can be that one with a vengeance.

## STONE CATCHERS

In his beautiful, heart-wrenching book *Just Mercy*, Bryan Stevenson, a lawyer dedicated to getting clients off death row, shared what an old church lady attending one of his trials said to him as he was leaving the courthouse. She was reflecting on the metaphorical stones people throw at each other, and she declared, "I decided that I was supposed to be here to catch some of the stones people cast at each other."[1]

I think there's a good chance, Two, that you're a stone catcher. Aren't you?

You've carried a lot of burdens that weren't yours to bear, huh? You hoisted millstones off other broken folks and onto your own shoulders, convincing yourself that you were the one whose back wouldn't break, didn't you? And somehow, against the odds, you're still here. Your back didn't break. You're a miracle, and so is your survival. But it's time to rest, darlin'. You do not have to break yourself to rebuild somebody else. That is no kind of justice. Your watch is over. It's time to rest. There are no dues to pay for the price of existing; there is no one you have to prove yourself to.

## WINGS

The wings available to a Two are One (the Machine) and Three (the Winner). While some wings vary wildly, the 2w1 and 2w3 have only subtle differences. Wing One, for example, brings a perfectionist's eye to the helpfulness of the Two: they wanna get it right, at all times. There's a more serious air to this wing type—they want to be the *MOST BEST* at whatever it is you need. They'll kick themselves

---

1. Bryan Stevenson, *Just Mercy: A Story of Justice and Redemption* (New York: Spiegel and Grau, 2014), 308.

for not getting it right or thinking of that thing you *obviously* needed first. Reminding a 2w1 that they're (a) doing enough and (b) just inherently enough on their own is key.

The Three wing brings a kind of double dose of image sensitivity to the Two. Sorry, kids, it's rough, I know! A 2w3 wants to be a helper but also to be *seen* as being a helper. A 2w3 is a consummate host, making sure everyone at the dinner party or the fundraising event is having the goddamn time of their lives. Anything their name is assigned to has to be just so.

When more integrated, 2w3s become champions of the downtrodden or marginalized, identifying needs no one else has noticed and deftly implementing strategies to go about tending to them. One of my fave 2w3s recognized that the teachers at her local elementary school didn't have the capital necessary to get all their students the supplies they needed, and she was incensed that the cost of these supplies had to come out of teachers' thinly lined pockets. In mere hours she orchestrated online fund-raisers and posted Amazon wish lists for the classrooms she sought to help.

## INSTINCTUAL VARIANTS

### Self-Preserving Twos

I call Self-Pres Twos the soccer moms. While their name hardly suggests it, they care for themselves the least but talk about it more. It seems to be a point of particular angst that Self-Pres Twos often can't stop wearing themselves ragged, and then they're pissed that they're ragged. *Why isn't anyone helping me? Could it be because I already told everyone that I had shit handled on my own?* Nah, couldn't be!

One dear Self-Pres Two I knew had a delightful little habit of reminding me constantly about everything she had done for me—the money she had spent, the sacrifices she had made, etc.—much as one would expect a mother to do. I think she hoped these dependable reminders would prompt ongoing gratefulness from me, when of course all they ended up doing was foster resentment and hostility to whatever help she offered me in the future. Talk about a vicious cycle!

## Social Twos

Social Twos have a significantly different approach. I mean, they're still on the whole Meet Others' Needs to Meet Mine train, buuuuut they seem to be more chill about it, on the surface. Social Twos, which I call the Indispensables, are hella social and hella connected. A Social Two never met a stranger, which is why they often get confused with Sevens, just purely based on behavior. (Again, however, the Enneagram is not about behavior; it's about motivation. We gotta get to the root of shit. Thank you, this has been a PSA.)

Social Twos are strategic about their social engagement, on a level that fun-loving, seat-flying Sevens could only imagine. These folks know who to be friends with, and when and why, and which events they need to show up to and who to invite over and who to spend Friday night out on the town with. They make it look easy and like it doesn't require thought, but if you follow the threads of a Social Two's life, you'll find a clear, if meandering, course.

They do want to be indispensable to their friends, but their constant expansion into new spaces and new friend groups is often about how useful these new people can make them feel. It all sounds super conniving all typed out like this, but Social Twos usually don't admit even to themselves how calculated their choices are, instead believing they're just having a grand old time and are just lucky in friends and connections.

## Sexual Twos

Sexual Twos are "true intimacy junkies," as Riso and Hudson call them.[2] (Hats off to you, Riso and Hudson—a millennial title before its time.) Instead of spreading themselves quite so thin, Sexual Twos tend to concentrate on particular and ongoing one-on-one relationships, feeling as though they can't seem to get enough of the person they've set their sights on. Friends and lovers often get the same level of heightened intensity from these Twos, and given

---

2. Don Richard Riso and Russ Hudson, *The Wisdom of the Enneagram* (New York: Bantam, 1999).

enough unhealth, Sexual Twos can start to spiral into obsessive, fixating behaviors. Ewww—am I right?

Y'all see *Ingrid Goes West*? In the film, this real bored and depressed girl (played by Aubrey Plaza) sees one of these California lifestyle model types on Instagram (read: hipster with money) and just stalks the fuck out of her, upending her entire life and several other people's lives in the process . . . not a cute look. She pours all her time and attention and resources into making this one person love her, convinced she needs to be best friends with her to be happy. Spoiler alert: shit does not go according to the dream.

In health, though, Sexual Twos can be vibrant, pure-hearted, committed partners and friends, fountains of attention and emotional labor, consumed with giving and receiving happiness from their nearest and dearest. You want a healthy Sexual Two in your corner, let me tell you what.

## HELPING YOU HELP YOURSELF: INTEGRATION AND DISINTEGRATION FOR THE TWO

When Twos integrate, they slowly find they have a massive amount of empathy to offer both themselves and the world around them. They *see* people, and most people just don't get seen this way. They also see themselves in a way no one else does—because odds are, they haven't allowed themselves to need much from others.

Integrating Twos have the capacity to sense what someone needs, at their core, and to offer them that thing, regardless of how it serves them. As the musician Ryan O'Neal of Sleeping at Last says in the beautiful song "Two," dedicated to this very Enneagram number, "I will love you without any strings attached." This expansive capacity for love is inside you right now, my Two friend. It's yours to access.

The closer you come to security, to believing yourself to be enough on your own, without any coattails to ride or folks to need you, the more you'll sense the wideness open within you. As you integrate to Four, you'll find that creating space for yourself creates space for others too. You cannot help others breathe if you're allowing your life, your responsibilities, and your obligations to strangle you.

If Twos are stone catchers, then a disintegrated Two is someone who finally realizes they have an arsenal of stones at their disposal, and fuck if there aren't a lot of assholes in life to lob them at! Remember, disintegration is the direction we move in during crisis, which is often a very pivotal and defining moment and should not be considered inherently bad. As emotional creatures, we humans tend to pendulum swing to the opposite end of a spectrum when we realize we've spent our entire lives completing the same cyclical pattern forever and ever amen. So Twos in disintegration go to full-blown fire-breathing Eights, switching to a fierceness that can feel off-putting to folks who have known them to be sweet and accommodating.

Don't shy away from your disintegration, babies. Disintegration is almost always an indicator that something about your life is not quite right. If anger is information, then a Two's disintegration is whole-ass education. Lean into that intuitive anger and use it to identify which of your own needs you've been ignoring, and experience what it is to advocate for yourself, maybe for the first time.

## PLAYING WELL WITH OTHERS: RELATING TO A TWO WHEN YOU AREN'T ONE

For a Two, other people's boundaries can kiiiiinda be just speed bumps, hurdles on the way to the goal of useful connection. Twos can infiltrate lives and create complicated friend networks at truly mind-boggling rates. You'd be, like, a touch weirded out if Twos weren't so goddamn kind and accommodating and thoughtful all the time. There's never a sense that they're trying to outshine or overshadow you; they just want you to need them while they help you shine.

The mazes of human interaction are second nature to these kids, and they're often at the finish line before you've even rounded the first bend, hollering at you to catch the fuck up. It's crucial for you to show Twos that you want and love THEM—regardless of what they can do for you, regardless of how they can help you. Obviously there's a balance here, because part of a Two receiving love is you accepting theirs. People who love Twos, though, can encourage them toward their Four integration, redirecting them toward prioritizing themselves. Hell, encourage a little selfishness! Mixing a little selfishness in for a martyr type tends to sort of neutralize both extremes. When you see a Two wearing themselves thin—and you will—lovingly yell at them to knock that shit off, clear their plate, and center themselves, because only when we're being our true selves can we build mutual, equitable relationships that are life-giving to everyone involved.

## YOU MATTER. FULL STOP.

Put simply, Twos, you do not get to earn your mattering.

Why?

Because it was never meant to BE earned. It is not even given. It can only be known and believed, and the source of that belief must come from deep inside you.

I know the question of what *you* need is almost annoying to you at this point—you've spent the majority of your life not asking that question, or at least not prioritizing the answer. So when folks tell you to "self-care" or some shit, the entire concept seems foreign and uninviting. While part of me says to get the fuck over it and, ya know, treat yo'self, the more integrated part of me knows there's a lot more there. Let's try to dig in a bit.

How do you figure out what you need? Well, sometimes a better question is "What can I eliminate?" When you've spent so long not listening to yourself, it's key to quiet down the din to hear the small, ragged, hoarse voice of your true self trying to make itself heard. You gotta shut everybody else up so you can hear that voice speaking, even if it's just for an hour a day. It's a bit like a muscle that has atrophied after long years of little use. Consider this your physical therapy. You belong to yourself, and you need reminding.

It's important to remember that emotional labor is essentially just active seeing. You have an innate ability to notice what others will not. You don't have to FIX things. You just have to see. When you create space for others to expand, you'll find there's more room for you too. The first recipient of your attention and love should be you. When you can hold the same space and pay the same attention to yourself that you would spend lavishly on someone else, that's the sweet spot honey. It's not some bullshit cliché that you have to put your own oxygen mask on first. It's literally the only way that ANYONE'S gets on. A lot of us were indoctrinated with the notion that if we take care of others, they will take care of us. That's a fucking utopia, a fantasyland that doesn't exist, and it's pretty selfish. You're looking out for number two as a roundabout way of looking out for number one.

Your love cannot be predicated on someone else's feelings about you. That's not love; that's business. By the same token, being loved cannot be your job. You shouldn't have to earn it, and you shouldn't need passive aggression to get what you need.

Good news! Love is yours for the creating, and you're singularly gifted at it, Twos. You have love dripping out of your mouths and down your fingers and radiating out of your eyes. You're all attention and memory, the ingredients of love itself.

Practice those Big Gestures on yourself. Make yourself beautiful things to eat, buy yourself vain little presents, and fucking take yourself out dancing. Whatever your thing is, feed it. Create a liturgy of self-affirmation to repeat to yourself when no one else will. Marinate in your own goddamn goodness. The self may be a made-up concept, but it's ours to make up!

And you know what else? You gotta speak up. Nobody is gonna read your mind or anticipate your needs, because chances are, they aren't Twos, yo! You can't hold your people responsible for not meeting needs you didn't articulate.

Don't wait on somebody else to tend or mend you. All that emotional labor you've been spending on other people—the blood, the sweat, the tears—belongs, first, to you. Hollow out the space you need in your own goddamn life. Chances are you've cluttered shit up real good. Air out your room, girl. Open the shades. Let your own light in.

I'M A
MILLENNEAGRAM
TWO, SO

CAN I GET
YOU A
REFILL?

# MILLENNEAGRAM
# 3

## THE WINNER

"

It's not bragging if it's true.

**HARVEY SPECTER, CHARACTER IN *SUITS***

HE WAS A STARRY SUMMER NIGHT OF A BOY, AND I WAS hooked. His name was John, and he was about to break my heart for the first time.

John was the kind of guy who lit up (I swear his eyes flashed like flames on steel) every time he spoke about something he gave a shit about, and he gave a shit about a lot of shit. He could walk into any room and leave it well noticed and well remembered. He could charm anything that moved and was the best at being, well, the best. I was seventeen and in love. The thing is, John was a few different boys all at once. He was one respectful boy to my parents (who kept a stern and watchful eye on him), another to me (all passion and tenderness and bad minimalist poems), and another boy entirely to his co-ed college dorm (getting around, if you know what I mean). John kept all the plates spinning masterfully, until one day he couldn't.

The plates fell to the ground when I found his dorm girlfriend on Facebook, whose profile pic showed him nestled in her neck with the caption "My boyfriend is amazing!"

I had been too love-drunk to see that he was playing a part with me, just like he'd played a part for my parents and for his college friends. John was your typical Three: smart, ambitious, eager to charm the pants off you, and, in this case, so adaptable in an effort to climb the social ladder that they become disingenuous.

It took me ten years to stop wishing different outcomes of first love for myself, but I finally realized he couldn't help himself. At their core, Threes wants to win whatever game they're playing, and if that game is a relationship, they'll project an image that will help them do that.

While John and I hardly had a happy ending, Threes at their healthiest know how to navigate their spaces and communities with emotional intelligence, presence, and a big ole dollop of charm.

## I'M NOT HERE TO PLAY—I'M HERE TO WIN

All right, Threes. Whattup?

Threes are troop ralliers. Shit handlers. They are artful but active, smooth but hardworking. I call this type the Winner because hustle is the name of their game. If there's a thing to be won, they're fucking going to. Threes are on some Olivia Pope "It's handled" shit. A key part of their survival story is the whole idea that love is for winners, and to win, you have to play the game. Several, in fact.

And to win a game, you need a solid game plan.

Often billed as arrogant, Threes are confident in the abilities they've put their blood, sweat, and tears into. Everything they win is hard earned. They know damn well nothing will be handed to them, so they've learned how to take what they need. Persuasive and dynamic, these folks can strategize effectively and inspire folks sufficiently toward a common end. Threes use their emotional intelligence to read other people quickly and accurately, and they can pick up on the nonverbal cues in a room faster than any other number. Often this ability leads to a chameleon effect, where Threes play whichever role is required or expected of them at any given moment.

Can I just get something off my chest? As a Four, I know a thing or two about being misunderstood. Folks throw a lotta words around for Threes, like "deceptive" and "slimy" and bullshit like that. Fact is, what you see is not necessarily what you get with Threes, and that frustrates the hell outta people. They make us nervous with their adaptability, their smoothness, and their poise.

Threes understand that different spaces and situations call for different approaches, different strokes. They're adept at managing the expectations of the subcultures they navigate: home, work, friend groups, family. Keeping all the balls in the air comes naturally to them, and let's face it, we're all lowkey jealous.

Situated in the dead center of the Feeling Triad, Threes are as concerned as Twos and Fours are with the way they're perceived by those around them, but where Twos want to be seen as helpful and supportive, occupying a kind of right-hand position to power, Threes seek to be the successful figures that Twos support.

## PASSION: DECEIT

There has been some debate through the years about which passion best describes the Three, with heavy hitters like Naranjo and Ichazo, originators of the Enneagram system, disagreeing about it. The myth that Threes are vain as fuck follows them through life, especially when people pick up on the whole "I'm projecting an image" thing. (I'll be honest, darlins. You're fooling us less than you think.)

Truth is, Threes take more pride in what they do than in who they are, and they're never really done. There's no resting on their laurels for them, literally no time to sit around and be vain!

The passion I think best describes the Three is deceit, because Threes are fake-it-till-you-make-it folks. They're usually not coming from a malicious place. Most Threes just kind of dive in and expect themselves to rise to the occasion. It's more like they show us what they WANT to be true about themselves. Unfortunately, sometimes what we want to believe about ourselves isn't the actual truth, is it?

Our survival stories, while commendable for getting us this far, always obscure our deepest, truest, and most expansive selves, and there's nobody this is more true for than our beloved Threes. The opposite of deceit is truthfulness, and truth is the greatest weapon in the Three's arsenal, and usually the least utilized. Habits are a bitch to break, and before Threes can start speaking the truth, they have to realize they aren't.

## SURVIVAL STORY: SET LIFE

Dearest Three, maybe you had an overexacting parent figure who had his or her own very unattainable idea of the person you needed to be, the goals you needed to attain, and the prizes you needed to win. Maybe you've just always been the kind of person who sets your own standards, competing with yourself for a level of success that is always deliciously one or two steps out of reach. Half the fun is the chase—am I right?!

The trouble with needing to win is that nobody wins all the time, and that's where the other half of the Three's survival story comes in. Survival stories are almost always a patchwork of half-truths that obscure from us the reality of our true selves. Being our truest self is not often a safe activity, and so each of us, in our own way, avoids it as best we can. And while all of us set up a sort of "ego ideal" for ourselves, as Maitri calls it in *The Enneagram of Passions and Virtues*, Threes are the only type who attempts to convince both themselves and those around them that they ARE that ideal. It's a tall order to fill, and 99 percent of the time Threes are up to the task.

Threes need to succeed, not for the power or the pleasure it can afford but because they're trying to swim upstream from a worthlessness they're sure awaits them if they should ever slow down. There's an unspoken desperation to stay a few strokes ahead of this dreaded precipice. There's no question of chilling out, because chilling out would mean achieving less, and their entire sense of self-worth is derived from accomplishing shit. Yes, I too am exhausted, just by writing that.

## CHAMELEON COMPLEX

Like chameleons, Threes are the shape-shifters of the Enneagram, masters of illusion and elusiveness. Freaking MAGICIANS, yo. Most of us suck at identifying exactly what level of professionalism is required in our current workplace or how to keep our families from clawing each other's faces off at reunions or what kind of friend our friend in crisis needs us to be right now. But Threes are on that shit, man. They slide seamlessly from room to room, strategizing about how to fit themselves into the expectation boxes each new interaction confronts them with. They want to mirror what you want to see in them. It's pretty fucking genius when you think about it.

What's sad, though, is that all of this shape-shifting makes it difficult for Threes to return home again—to themselves and to their own bodies. They often lose the ability to differentiate between their true selves and the presentations they have created. Now, what I refuse to do is use the word "mask" here, because I think it's an unfair descriptor of this kind of scrappy versatility we find in Threes, pegging them as sort of criminal masterminds, conning everyone around them. Let's be real: we all play these games with one another, because (a) it's easier and (b) our Western-ass capitalist society finds our true selves mad inconvenient. Don't hate on Threes just cause they're better at it. They've had to become so to survive.

My friend Josh puts it this way:

Though I knew that I had lived as a chameleon for most of my life (becoming all things to all people at the cost of never developing a sense of self), I discovered a new depth of revelation—that I had no semblance of character or personal value that lived in my bones. Anything good, moral, and right about how I was living my life was built like a Hollywood set that looked beautiful from the outside, but once you walked through the door, you'd discover there's nothing behind it. I had taken an easier path with my life [by discovering] what someone else wanted me to be and mimicking those behaviors rather than doing the work to explore the kind of person I wanted to become.

As Josh discovered, when they're at their most unhealthy, there's no one more conned than the Threes themselves.

Downtime is a freaking myth for most Threes. There is no point at which they're done DOING, and rest of any kind brings up uncomfortable and inconvenient feelings that slow productivity and throw a wrench in their well-oiled machine. Despite being at the center of the Feeling Triad, Threes are perhaps the most obviously removed from their inner life, fooling amateur onlookers into thinking they don't have much of one. Truth is, creating and maintaining the correct presentations to engage with each of their social spheres is a helluva lot of emotional labor. They're too busy seducing feels out of other people to feel much themselves.

The cool and trippy thing about the Enneagram, though, is that the opposite of each type's weakness is their strength. I know, a mind fuck, huh? So, at their highest level of health, Threes can convince themselves to occasionally take a vacation from doing and just be. Being of course requires not only seeing oneself clearly—which all the fucking motion of their doing conveniently blurs—but also communicating what one finds within to the people who matter. It's a tall order, I know, but, hey, ya got your whole life to get there.

## WINGS

The difference between the Two wing (the Parent) and the Four wing (the Tortured Artist) has a lot to do with the spheres of influence that the particular Three in question seeks to occupy. 3w2s are far more likely to blend their Three and Two interests in the personal/relationship area of their lives, while 3w4s focus more on what they create, produce, and release into the world—their "professional" lives.

My internet friend Eli, a 3w2, uses most of her Three charm in her relationships. (Internet friends are real friends, okay? Don't @ me.) She and her two best friends like to get all dolled up and have date nights doing CAPA (conversation as performance art) at local bars. What a concept! I love it because it so perfectly encapsulates the performance and projection of the Three as well as the Two's need for consistent friendship maintenance. Party on, Eli. I'm gonna crash this shit sometime.

3w4s, on the other hand, seem more concerned with what they put out into the world and the impact it has. When I was designing my Millenneagram wing mugs, my friend Mandy, a 3w4, wrote in to suggest that the 3w4 mug say "I'm a 3w4 and I'm full of articulate rage." 3w4s fuse their natural affinity for strategic decisions with their creativity, and right in that sweet spot is where the magic happens. They have the ability to produce something unique and sell the fuck out of it. An unhealthy 3w4 could probably sell butter to cows.

**115**

## INSTINCTUAL VARIANTS

### Self-Preserving Threes

All right, so a reminder: having an instinctual subtype doesn't always mean a person is particularly good at that thing—like, just because Self-Pres Threes are concerned with survival doesn't mean they're good at self-care. Ya feel me? Self-Pres Threes are the Threes whose standards are most obvious, which means they might remind you of a One from time to time. Self-Pres Threes care about actually being as good or as effective as the ego ideal they present to you, which means that workaholism is a massive symptom of this sub-type. These are the Threes most removed from their feelings, since they view any part of themselves that is not invested in the task at hand as superfluous.

I always think about Harrison Ford's iconic Linus Larrabee in the remake of *Sabrina*. You remember the one, right? Rich boys, a fierce-ass makeover, and a romantic triangle? In Linus, we have a Three so invested in maintaining his empire that he leaves himself no time to actually sit back and enjoy it. Here's a dude who has everything going for him in the business world—he's committed, goal oriented, and pretty fuckin' cutthroat when he needs to be—marrying his brother off for mergers and shit! The only things he doesn't have are love and friendship and emotional engagement—all right, there's a lot he doesn't have. Sabrina sorts him out pretty good, and reminds him that he's a human with feelings, and how existing without experiencing and expressing them is half a life, at best. I have feelings about the idea that a romantic relationship can solve all of one's character flaws, but hey. I'm a sucker for a good fairy tale every now and then.

## Social Threes

It's fascinating, the ways in which one Enneagram type can look so wildly different based on what seem like small, inconsequential tweaks. Social Threes, while programmed with similar motivations as Self-Pres Threes, could not look more different. Social Threes seem to have an almost superhuman radiance, shining in every situation they find themselves in. They're more obviously good with people than their more serious Self-Pres counterparts. Their natural charm and easy grace makes them look like Sevens from time to time, but the underlying image consciousness of the Feeling Triad sits just under the surface for these kids too.

Social Threes are natural social climbers, freaking ladder demolishers, cats with nine lives who always seem to land on their feet after a setback. Maybe it's karma. Maybe it's Maybelline. It's definitely a Social Three.

## Sexual Threes

As with all sexual subtypes, the Sexual Three is less worried about big-picture workplace or big-picture people but focuses on becoming the perfect partner, the perfect friend, or the perfect teammate. They thrive in one-on-one situations and tend to set more relational goals

**117**

than vocational. They're more emotionally reactionary than the other two subtypes but still fairly disconnected from their true selves in unhealth. A healthy Sexual Three is going to be the best boo, though.

## REMEASURING SUCCESS: INTEGRATION AND DISINTEGRATION FOR THE THREE

When Threes move toward the healthiest version of themselves, they usually integrate into Six, which invites them to reconnect with the present—to allow themselves a break from doing or leading and just BE. Threes are often so busy DOING their lives that they forget to experience their lives. Finding out that they don't have to handle everything all the time can feel like a punishment or a relief—and sometimes it's both. A Three might work right up to the edge of what their body and brain can handle or until control is taken away from them by an outside force. For example, a Three might lose a job that was making them frazzled or meet someone who reminds them that there is more to life than achieving.

I wanna return to the whole Linus Larrabee example, mostly because I'm too lazy to think of another movie character. Y'all can deal. The point is, Sabrina Fairchild finds some fucking self-love and waltzes back into Linus Larrabee's life with her collection of fashionable hats and a breezy joy that charms him into stepping away from his high-powered corporate life and multimillion-dollar wheeling and dealing to get reacquainted with himself. He remembers that he loves to sail; he takes her to his old childhood home, and you can almost watch his shoulders release, even as he is comically frustrated with himself for this release of tension. Spoiler alert (it's a twenty-year-old movie—you're fine): he finds that he's the sort of person to book last-minute flights to Paris to go find the woman he loves! He finally takes a break from winning and starts actually living, and he finds there is no substitute for true love and true self. He spends most of the movie surprising himself, and it is a sight for sore eyes.

Emotions are messy, and far from strategic. This is challenging for Threes, who have learned to take life full steam ahead, rising to endless occasions and probably wearing the fuck out of their bodies in the process. Ultimately, though, avoidance doesn't solve shit; it only prolongs it. The feelings we stifle are still there, stored in our bodies, waiting for their moment to be expressed and released.

Sleeping at Last, in the song "Three," captures this moment so succinctly: "I finally see myself, unabridged and overwhelmed." All of the heart types—Twos, Threes, and Fours—have a habit of abridging themselves to fit the narrative they're trying to tell. But being human is messy and multidimensional. All of us contain multitudes, and we often don't see this within ourselves until a moment of crisis makes us temporarily disintegrate.

Integrating to Six can be a crucial moment of pause for a Three—to turn some of that emotional intelligence back on themselves and do the very brave, big thing of seeing what the fuck is going on inside. Rediscovering oneself can sometimes feel like a crisis—like encountering an overgrown secret garden that has gone untended for so long it's difficult to know where even to begin.

In stress, Threes disintegrate to Nine. All of a sudden their hyperactivity crawls to a screeching halt, and their bodies and brains shut down and retract, which can feel like the end of the world to a Three. But not all crises are bad. Everybody needs a solid dark night of the soul now and then. Crises are defining moments, turning points that present us with the choice to continue on autopilot or to plot a new course. You can imagine which option we go with most of the time. We're creatures of habit, after all. Crises give us a chance to look around and be like *Wait, did I pick this shit? Is this me? Am I headed toward wholeness or am I treading water here?* We avoid these moments because they scare up in us feelings that make us rather uncomfortable. In order to grow, though, we have to let go of our preconceived notions of ourselves and lean into the questions that feel most impossible to ask.

A Three disintegrating to Nine suddenly has a chance to slow down and take stock of their life—to look around and say, *Am I actively choosing this, or am I continuing to play a role or win a game that has no value to me anymore?* If you're a Three (or any other type, frankly) and you meet that question with honesty and full presence—without avoidance or grandstanding—the answer will meet you. Your life will thank you.

## PLAYING WELL WITH OTHERS: RELATING TO A THREE WHEN YOU AREN'T ONE

Here's a common interaction between Threes and non-Threes: non-Threes say something, Threes nod and say, "Hmm," while also scanning stations on the radio, operating a vehicle, and chowing down on dinner without missing a beat . . . and the non-Three asks, "Are you listening?!"

A really cool big word that experts use to describe a Three's activity style is "polyphasic," which essentially just means Threes are dyed-in-the-wool multitaskers. We're not talking the kind of multitasking where you *were* writing a paper and got just a li'l off track bingeing Netflix and rearranging your sock drawer. We're talking full-attention, full-tilt, next-level multitasking.

As a result, it can feel like a Three is not giving you their full attention, because full attention to most people looks like eye contact, empty hands, and general stillness. We don't expect that someone can be taking in what we're saying while moving at lightning speed through all their daily chores. Although there's a good chance your Three is actually cataloging everything you're saying, it's okay to say, "Hey, buddy, objectively I know that you are, but could you, like, stop for a sec so it can LOOK like you're listening to me?" I mean you'll probably say it better, but you catch my drift.

Getting steamrolled by a Three is kind of a rite of passage. Have you ever offered up an innovative opinion during a team meeting

**121**

at work and been met with a very polite "Thanks so much for your suggestion, but it's [say it with me] handled!" Kind of a Three move. It's very rarely consciously done; it's just that Threes can do more than you in less time and are probably about five steps ahead of you in terms of strategy. It's almost never a malicious move, but Threes just don't put much stock in your individual hang-ups, concerns, or straight-up laziness. It doesn't matter to them who does something as long as it gets done, but usually they just happen to be the ones ready to do that something first.

Similar to Twos, Threes need to be reminded that succeeding at a relationship—winning at it, if you will—requires showing up as your whole self, which starts with admitting to yourself who that is. Any emotional labor you bring to the table outside the self is just fucking busywork, honey.

## COME HOME, BOO

For the Three who has long since tuned out the voice of your true self—the self who sits deep within all of us, underneath the frosting of personality, the bit of us that some folks call "the soul"—it's crucial to create room in that shouty headspace of yours for your voice to come back. She might be a bit shy at first. She might be a LOT shy at first. Coax her back. Reward her for making herself heard, and celebrate those victories—the little day-to-day decisions you make that honor her, regardless of whether or not it fits well with your image.

Hearing is a muscle we all gotta flex more often. Those obnoxious twins Avoidance and Numbing will work hard to make you listen less. It's important not to get into a fistfight with them. Rather, thank them for the role they've played in getting you this far, and let them know graciously that you've got it from here.

Though, as the poet Nayyirah Waheed said, "take your time. You are coming home to yourself."[1] It's often a long journey. Take snack breaks.

We get it. You got stuff to do. Places to see. People to be. You've been honing your skills for a long time—you know this shit is a long con. You probably have a timeline laid out, or maybe you're just relying on your raw intuition to get you there. You've got this.

But do you got YOU?

Ultimately no recognition, no validation, no trophies or achievements or employee-of-the-fucking-month plaques will earn you value. There is no rubric for being good enough, and there is no "arrival." We all have one journey, this little adventure of existing in our little space and our little sphere of influence on our little twirling shit planet right now. There are no arbitrary or objective designations of worth that matter. You received permission to exist simply by existing, and the only person who can assign you any meaning is you.

---

1. Nayyirah Waheed, *Salt* (San Bernardino, CA: Create Space, 2013).

What a fucking tragedy it would be if you spent your whole adventure avoiding the only voice that really matters in the end.

Chances are, my dear baby Three, you're still gonna be a hotshot. You're still gonna be kind of a big deal. The shining is not the problem. All I'm concerned with is that the shining is true—that the person we're charmed and mesmerized and a bit overwhelmed by is the real you. I want to see her looking out of your eyes. I want to hear him laugh.

Don't let anyone tell you that you need to be smaller to be healthy. That's some first-rate medal-winning horseshit right there. Take up all that goddamn space, honey! What's a band without a front man? Hell, for that matter, what's a band without a manager? The world needs entrepreneurs and dreamers, strategists and diplomats. The world needs pastors and priests, prophets and pep talkers. There's a lot of Big Bad that needs undoing, and there will always be room for your voice. Helluva lotta folks will be content just to follow you, sidekick you, do your bidding, and just generally bask in your glow.

Take the mic, my good bitch, or take the reins. Just make sure the voice you use sounds like you and no one else.

I'M A MILLENNEAGRAM THREE, AND

**ALL I DO IS WIN.**

# MILLENNEAGRAM
# 4

## THE TORTURED ARTIST

**66**

Talent is insignificant.
I know a lot of talented ruins.

JAMES BALDWIN,
*THE PARIS REVIEW INTERVIEWS, II*

WHEN I WAS A LITTLE GIRL, I DISCOVERED A WEIRD PROCLIV-
ity for limes. We moved to Mexico when I was six, and limes were
served with everything. It became a personal challenge for me to
eat both the spiciest things I could stomach and as many limes as I
could. It got to where I could eat dozens of them in one sitting. The
Mexican kids thought I was nuts, but there are worse vices, right? I
used to shove every wedge between my teeth and squeeze it as hard
as I could, coming back to each piece of dry rind again and again to
make sure I got every last sour drop.

That's what Fours do with FEELINGS. We suck those feelings
dry, coming back to them over and over again in our imaginations to
evoke new meaning or to try to get that same high we felt before. It's
beautiful in many ways because we Fours are empathetic, creative, and
able to see shit from angles y'all have never DREAMED of. It's also
a curse because introspection on that level is completely exhausting.

We Fours also mistakenly believe that our problems will be
solved in our imaginations, where we play out possible conversations
as though they were happening in real time. The other thing I did
as a kid was think about a feeling so hard that it tied my cheeks up
in knots and pushed tiny crocodile tears out of my eyes. My sister

would laugh and point and yell at my mom that I was faking, and in a way, she was right. In another, she wasn't. I knew the emotion that needed out was lurking just below the surface, with every intention of bothering me at the most inconvenient fucking moments. Forcing pathetic Tiny Tim tears to the surface when I needed them seemed like the only way to reset my internal equilibrium.

Turns out that's not unlike how I process emotions as an adult. I have whole exchanges with friends and lovers in my head, trying to imagine their exact responses and my reactions to those responses. It's like grown-up dress-up, because I get to try on different moods and intonations and dramatic pauses until I get just right what I would say in the exact instance I'm fantasizing about . . . even though the chances are that exact encounter will never happen.

Unfortunately, this sort of useless narration is exactly what a Four's brain starts to do in the wake of any emotionally significant moment in their life. Not relying on the wisdom of the body to guide them where they need to go, the Four crawls up into their imagination to second-guess themselves and everyone else involved in that moment until reality is just a distant memory.

## THE SWEET TORTURE OF ART

Well, fuck. I hate to say it, but there isn't a better term for an Enneagram Four than Tortured Artist. They're master feelers, using emotional intelligence to create whole worlds of fancy and fantasy, often parallel with or intertwining with the real one, where their imaginations can run wild. Fiery, passionate, naturally creative—even those of us who have never picked up a pen or a brush are creators in our own right, whether we're designing our living spaces, our experiences, or our aesthetic. Oh, and we're tortured as shit too. Early on, we Fours internalized the message that we were voted off the island, estranged from the rest of humankind somehow, and that our uniqueness keeps us from a normal and happy life. In the same breath, however, we are relieved to be abnormal, to be on the outskirts of things, because this separation solidifies our specialness for us.

But, honey, let's not play. We eat that shit up. Being different is our fucking calling card.

Enneagram teacher Helen Palmer has called Fours "too precious for ordinary life,"[1] and while I'm very offended and we're definitely in a fight, I can't say I disagree. Fours have unrealistic expectations not only of our friends and relationships but also of life. When life fails to take our breath away, to surprise us, to awe us and inspire us, we create our own magic or melancholy.

Trouble with that is, when we start playing make-believe, we lose the authenticity we so dearly crave.

---

1. Helen Palmer, *The Enneagram in Love & Work: Understanding Your Intimate & Business Relationships* (San Francisco: HarperOne, 1995), 12.

## FOURS AND CREATIVE ENERGY

The lie Fours often believe about creativity is this: that there is a finite quantity of it out there in the world. That once used, it's spent. The myth of scarcity runs deep in Western culture.

But creativity is a renewable resource, and you don't have to be its source—you're merely the conduit. Take that fucking weight off your shoulders, fellow Fours. Creativity is a fickle mistress, and her guidance is not easily mapped or charted. Whether she gives you a poem or a billion-dollar business idea, go ahead and just make the dang thing. Don't dwell on it, turning it over and over in your hands until it makes more sense to you. Don't wait until you can comfortably fit it into your overactive and ever-revising sense of self.

I know that sometimes it's easier to think about doing a thing or imagining doing a thing or reminiscing on the goddamn thing you made three YEARS ago than putting your hand to the plow and making your shit now. But that's a tired story. Write a new one.

Make the thing. Release it. Rinse. Repeat.

Send your darlings out into the world to, like, get a job and shit. They're grown now. Go make some more.

## PASSION: ENVY

Fours believe, somewhere deep down, that they were handed the short stick in life. On some level, Fours tend to think they're perhaps unique, but also uniquely lacking. The passion of envy rears its head as they look around at their peers and family and friends and think, *Well, fuck. Everybody else is hella normal and seems to be relatively happy. What code are they speaking in? What secret do they hold? What am I missing out on?*

This perceived sense of lack often causes Fours to feed illusions of grandeur—shit like *Nobody understands me because I'm in fact above them and a genius.* Casual. The lie of scarcity affects all humans, but in Fours it's particularly acute. While turning up their noses at the boring clichés of the masses, Fours secretly yearn for the sense of belonging others seem to experience that they never can. But quiet as it's kept, melancholy is a sweet, sweet drug. It's possible sometimes to feed yourself with hunger and soothe yourself with longing.

## SURVIVAL STORY: FANTASY WORLDS

The not-belonging starts early for Fours. They often grow up feeling like the odd one out in their families—as if dropped there by mistake. Like my friend Ally, they are often told that their feelings are too much or too deep or—worst of all—inconvenient. Their disillusionment with the real makes Fours grow up in the rich fantasy swamps of imagination.

Within the wilds of parallel universes, a Four searches for their lost self, expecting to find it somewhere outside their body and their present. This looks a bit different from person to person. Some Fours tinker with their past history, imagining different outcomes and getting lost in precious old feelings that still feel valuable to them. Other Fours play with fantasy futures, trying on different cities and careers and relationships in their minds, imagining what it would feel like to be there or feel that or kiss them. The present is lost in the what-could-be and the what-could-have-been.

A perfect example is represented in my favorite movie, which I'm almost afraid to admit to y'all cause it's almost too cliché and, like, I'm unique, bitch. Okay?! Nevertheless, my favorite movie is *Amelie*, a story of a well-meaning young woman who has had to retreat into her imagination in order to keep herself company. She embarks on all these little good-doing missions in order to actually help others but also to create the ideal self she imagines in her mind. Even as she almost gets lost in the weeds of her fantasies, love finds her and moors her to the present. No spoilers, babes, but watch that shit.

## WINGS

Fours have a Three wing (the Winner) and a Five wing (the Detective). 4w3s are natural creators, but their audience is always in mind. They think, *Who's going to see this and how will they respond to it?* They also feel very strongly that they have to be producing constantly, that there is no time and they have never done enough. They're full of what I call "performative angst"—the angst is real, but, like, they need someone to see and acknowledge it. *I just need to know that I am SEEN and that somebody fuckin' gets it, okay?! Is that so much to ask?!*

At first glance, 4w5s display more like Fives. They're more measured, more thoughtful, less extra. They do a lot of research into their interests and potential creative projects. And 4w5s are deeply creative people, but they often mistake talking about creativity or researching their creativity for actually making something. Before they know it, five years have gone by and they're still deciding how to get started on the thing. The Five wing lends a visceral need to be all the way prepared, to have all of one's ducks in a row before making a move.

4w5s are often more visibly melancholic—think Jughead in the thriller-soap *Riverdale*. They've got a playlist for every emotion. Their fantasy worlds are more brilliant and detailed than the harebrained 4w3s—they are deep wells of beauty and feeling. In the Five chapter, I talk about the "mind palace" concept, expanded on for the BBC detective series *Sherlock*. Where Fives have thought palaces, Fours have feeling palaces. Imagine the awe-inspiring things a person could create with both! Epic storytellers like J. R. R. Tolkien and J. K. Rowling come to mind, spinning entire universes of lore and creating equally gripping protagonists. Consider yourself lucky if a 4w5 invites you inside their mind for a tour.

## INSTINCTUAL VARIANTS

### Self-Preserving Fours

More masochistic than obviously dramatic, Self-Pres Fours enact the Four passion of envy by hustling to gather things for themselves—whether it be something concrete, like the right house or car, or more abstract, like the attention of a soul mate—that will fill the emotional void they experience. They're less aware of their feelings of envy than the other subtypes—they just think they're working hard to get the things they want, much like Ones and Threes. Where Threes will usually acquire or achieve what it is they want, Self-Pres Fours often end up sabotaging themselves in one way or another. Their drama is in squashing their feelings down. A man I once loved who was a Self-Pres Four was in the habit of saying "It's too late for me" when I asked him about his creative endeavors because he had, like, a nice-paying job and hadn't spent his twenties gallivanting around as a starving artist. My response was always "You're not dead yet, so I don't wanna hear it." Hey, Self-Pres Four? You're not dead yet, so I don't wanna hear it.

Self-Pres Fours also tend to make snap decisions with their money, career, or relationships—if they sense that something is not quite right, they aren't above making dramatic moves to change shit up. This is not at all like that time I felt my life was becoming too normal so I quit my job and moved across the country to Nashville to date a man I barely knew and work for a band I had loved from afar. Not like that at all.

## Social Fours

Social Fours are the most outwardly histrionic of the bunch, often broadcasting their hardships to get the sympathy they feel they deserve. The victim complex is strong with these kiddos. Whereas all Fours are wallowers on some level, Social Fours like to wallow publicly, bringing others into their stories of suffering. Every Four at some point has used a vulnerable story of pain as social capital: *If I make you feel close to me, I'll get something I want from you.* It's a tried-and-true method, no shame in the game, but it can create quite the fucking brain rut. Instead of believing in themselves and their ability to dig themselves out, they can become comfortable with flailing for help and never quite getting helped all the way.

There's also a bit of an inferiority complex thing going on with Social Fours. Fours in general sort of believe they're uniquely fucked in some way, that the universe dealt them a short stick, and they look at the rest of the world through a glass darkly. Social Fours also often feel a sense of shame about the differences they perceive between themselves and the people they want to be connected with. Unfortunately, we all see what we want to see, and crying "Rejection!" all the time can turn into a self-fulfilling prophecy.

## Sexual Fours

Every time I hear "Dance Yrself Clean" by LCD Soundsystem, I laugh to myself at the line "Killing it with close inspection," because we Sexual Fours literally are. We are killing our attachments with attention. It's like overwatering your house plants (a thing I have definitely never done, by the way). We just want to see our relationships grow up big and strong. As children, we often experienced formative connections or precious adolescent friendships fall apart, and this only makes us more anxious about feeding our adult ones enough.

But what if love and connection aren't actually as hard as we imagine?

Look, hear me out. Most personality types require significant growth in their relational communication, when nine times out of ten, Sexual Fours could actually stand to tone it down. Your sibling or BFF or partner doesn't need to know every damn feeling that flits across your emotional landscape at any given time, and honestly, you don't either. Emotional intelligence requires an ability to sort one's emotions selectively, not express them indiscriminately whenever the self-disclosure bug strikes. There's a time to speak and a time to shut up, a time to feel and a time to observe that feeling without judgment and let it pass right the fuck on through.

## FROM TORTURED TO ARTIST: INTEGRATION AND DISINTEGRATION FOR THE FOUR

The Four moves to One in security, which means that all the time you spent daydreaming is time you now get to spend dOiNg tHiNGs! I know, crazy, huh?! Ones kinda hate downtime, but I think you'll find that your new motivation feels less like hyperactivity and more like a steady trudge in a pleasant direction. I don't wanna hear any hand-wringing bullshit about how you're the one Four who isn't an artist, okay? Because designing your life is your job now. Congratulations, motherfucker: you're an artist.

Spontaneity was fun and has its place, but it's time to plan, girl! Buy yourself a cool planner that fits your aesthetic—I promise you'll use it now. Your newfound One energy will thank you. It will feel a little weird and stilted at first, trying to get strategic with your life when you're used to being blown here and there and all around by the winds of your feels, but you got this. WE got this.

Suddenly realizing that you're right about a lot of shit will make you a bit of a grouch, because the world is a tremendously fucked-up place and a lot of people are running around being idiots on purpose. Lean into it. Grouches get shit done. They know what advice to reject and who to excise from their life. They know what they know, what they believe, and where they belong. There's a place for the rainbow lens with which you view the world, and there's a time to know what you know. Integration to One will help you to stand firm in the shit that is you and irrefutable.

And that's the fun and hard thing: you belong wherever you decide you do, baby girl. You are the only one who decides you're not an outsider anymore. You belong wherever the fuck you wanna be. It's your call. Stay outside the places that seek to diminish you, and wear that scarlet *A* with pride—then turn around and open the door you need opened. Don't wait for an invitation or for permission. You won't get either.

When Fours disintegrate to Two, we begin to use emotional engagement as a subtle manipulation tool to get the attention we don't think we're getting. A lot of us withdraw from our relationships in some respect, hoping that our absence will be noticed, and when it isn't, we passive-aggressively start hitting up all our friends to remind them what shitty friends they're being for not pursuing us. We'll start to fake being a present friend and "Oh, tell me about YOU," or we'll take on martyr roles nobody asked of us in the first place just to solidify our feelings of entitlement about receiving love and connection. Our desperation for real and positive connection ends up making us get a tad bit coercive with our friends and loved ones: "Whyyyyy aren't you showing yourself to me? Why do you never ask me questions about myself?" Yiiiiikes—am I right?

Disintegration is information. Instead of judging yourself for your neediness or spiraling, learn to take notice of the situations that bring out this desperation in you. Ask yourself questions in those moments: *How did I get here? What need am I feeling? How can I meet this need myself instead of relying on someone else to do it for me?*

When I was twenty-five, my husband left me. On Christmas we broke up, and on January 2 he had a new home. All my fears of abandonment became real in that moment, and I spent the next couple of years clinging to whichever friend could be bothered to watch me cry into gin and tonics at the bar and trying to fill the husband hole in my life with any trifling connection I could throw at it.

Once I realized this was me disintegrating to Two, I understood that no amount of friends or casual dates or wishful thinking could fill the husband hole left in my life. Nobody could do it but me. I resented the shit out of this for a while, because I was raised to believe that if I took care of everyone else, they would take care of me. Prioritizing my own care felt selfish and wrong. Nevertheless, little by little, I took baby steps in my own direction: choosing my mental health instead of another night out; choosing therapy and Zoloft over gin; choosing to redirect the loving energy I was spending on others on myself first, so when I did reach out to the people I loved, I did so without expectation or condition. Crisis is a bitch, but it pointed the way to growth for me, and it can for you too. Trust the process, honey. Sometimes you have to be demolished in order to rebuild a truer you.

## PLAYING WELL WITH OTHERS: RELATING TO A FOUR WHEN YOU AREN'T ONE

The flip side of envy is self-confidence, a deep and abiding belief that you are enough, just the way you are. For us Fours, a lot of this confidence comes from feeling *seen*, and hefty doses of thoughtful, specific affirmation are the fuel that keeps our engines running. We are easy to please, but we like to be often pleased. Tell us something about us that nobody else would notice. Give us a compliment that couldn't be given to anyone else. Intuit a need of ours—like, say, for example, super hypothetically, iced coffee first thing in the morning—and we'll be yours forever.

Show a Four that you get it by listening well and reflecting back what you hear—there is no drug like being understood, yo! Make us feel seen without feeding the vicious cycle of self-absorption that tells us no one can or does.

It also helps to give your favorite Four some fucking outlets! Don't let us sit on our hands and pine for a life that will give us meaning. Put pens and paper and tools in our hands, give us a solid shove out the front door, and make us go do something. We wallow in possibility forever. Make us face the now. We may complain in the moment, but we'll thank you later.

We need a fair bit of firm love too, though. I don't say "tough love" because I think it's a shit term that has been used to describe people saying cruel, true-ish things in a manner deeply unhelpful, and that's the opposite of what a Four needs. We need gentleness and patience, but we need to know you're not going to stand for this whole "outsider" charade we have going on. It's a deeply rooted belief that we have, and it will take some doing to get rid of, so consider it a long con. Tell us that we're an integral part of the family or the team or the friend group. Invite us to stick around.

## GO MAKE SHIT

Here's the deal, Fours: your life is happening all around you right now, and you're MISSING it. Wake the fuck up! You're so busy trying to resuscitate old feelings that you're allowing no space for the new ones and they're passing you by. I know that feelings you've felt in the past feel more precious than whatever is to come, and you're up in the hospital room, tryna revive and resuscitate that shit. DNR, BITCH.

I understand that the future is not dependable and, regardless of how miserable and crushing, the old feelings are. You know what that shit's going to do to you. You know exactly what those feelings feel like, how they affect you, how they turn you upside down and inside out. They will do in a pinch, when growth is too uncomfortable. But here's the truth: the stories you've been telling yourself are not serving you anymore. It's time to thank them and send them on their way.

They've kept you alive, but now you do. You keep you alive.

The other cool thing about your emotions is that they don't need your babysitting. The wisdom of your body is a thing you can ignore but not a thing you can override. Letting go of your iron-fisted control over your emotions will help you realize that they will go on existing, just a tad more quietly. And, Jesus, do you ever need the silence.

Resign yourself to the idea that YOU will be the person that "gets" you better than anyone else. You're not waiting on some bullshit soul mate. It sounds like a letdown, especially 'cause I said "resign," but I promise you it isn't. You have a built-in soul mate who follows you everywhere you go—someone who will keep you devoted company if you give her a chance. Everyone else will fall short, because your emotions are a function of your body and you're the only one who lives there.

Fours, you have always been so afraid of not belonging, and as it turns out, you don't! Your worst fears have been confirmed! You used to tell yourself that you didn't fit in so you wouldn't have to be faced with the actual objective truth of not fitting in. It's like breaking up with someone before they can break up with you. But there's something strangely soothing about one's worst fears being confirmed: it means there's nothing left to fear. You're free. When life has done its worst by you, when it has taken everything, all your veils and masks and pretty distractions, then you'll see yourself for who you really are, and you'll bask in the glory of your un-belonging. You'll create new spaces, the sort where people like you fit, and in so doing, you'll learn to look outside yourself. Because the grand joke of it all is that your uniqueness, your glorious individuality, is what keeps you from belonging, but in that space within yourself, you'll always matter. You'll always have a home.

Mr. Rogers once said, "Anything that's human is mentionable, and anything that is mentionable can be more manageable."[2] Our feel-

---

2. Fred Rogers, *Life's Journeys According to Mister Rogers: Things to Remember Along the Way* (New York: Hyperion, 2005).

ings are both mentionable and manageable. Repressing them does no good, but we have to manage them rather than let them manage us. Once we learn how to navigate them effectively, listening to the insight they give us and soothing the chaos they bring, we can leave tortured behind and truly become the artists and creators of our world.

Being at home with ourselves requires less histrionic outreach and more mundane maintenance: feeding ourselves, clothing ourselves, taking good care of our bodies, and creating the physical spaces that will both soothe and recharge us. Sounds boring, I know, but stick with yourself and stick with me. We're not disembodied souls, and we're not accidents. Making ourselves our home requires presence, which means digging ourselves out of the past and the future and allowing ourselves to just be, here, now, small and flawed and human. Now is all we've got.

I'M A
MILLENNEAGRAM
FOUR, AND

I'M DEEPER
THAN YOU.

# EACH

# TYPE

# IN

# TRAFFIC

## Ones

Well, if I can leave the house by 6:38, I should be able to arrive by 7:15, and Jesus, fuck, of course there was a wreck on the 10. I hate my life. Must tweet a picture of this traffic right now and my extreme displeasure at this incorrect behavior on the part of the world at large.

## Fours

Well, at least my melancholic piano playlist and mesmerizing podcast queue are on point so I can be learning things and feeling beautiful things on the way. What is life, after all, but a highway that leads us on endlessly to places unknown . . . ?

## Sevens

Oh please that's not a beer, that's a new kombucha I HAD to try and like . . . let's be real I'm already late so it's no big deal. WHY DON'T I do a bold eye shadow and eat this breakfast sandwich while belting my fave songs and paying little or no attention to the actual road and miraculously still arrive intact.

## Twos

OMG, I should get over, OMG, but I'll let them go. I mean, what can I say? I'm a NICE person, okay? Jesus, these assholes. Not sure what I even signal for. (*Swerves, causing mass panic in the back seat.*) It's not like anyone else bothers to be CONSIDERATE.

## Threes

I shall use this time wisely! I shall make important phone calls! I shall put on a bold lip! I shall upload an Instagram Live of me pontificating on important knowledge! Fuck a traffic jam. I'm going places PARKED, bitch.

## Fives

Can't let anyone see how anxious this is making me right now. I must fake certainty that this is the correct direction, because I know everything, obviously. Fuck. It's gonna take me a whole afternoon to recover from this emotional expenditure occurring deep below my surface.

## Sixes

IS THIS or IS THIS NOT the right way? I did not like going this way last time, it made me carsick, and I refuse to get carsick. Hi—I need you to employ your GPS and your internal compass and, I don't know, your fucking Rand McNally ATLAS right now, bitch, and get me on the right path here.

## Eights

Fuck these motherfuckers (*indiscriminate middle fingers*). I'll show YOU road rage, bitch. Pipe down back there. I'm deeply unconcerned about getting shot up by racist gun toters on this road right now. Just shut up and let me handle this, honey.

## Nines

WHAT traffic, honestly. I am oblivious, this is fine, I'm zen as fuck, I 100% dare this traffic to upset my equilibrium and I also 100% dare this bitch to backseat drive me right now, hell nah. Nothing and no one is escalating in this vehicle YOU HEAR ME!?

# THE
# THINKING
# TRIAD

# PART III

# BRAIN KIDS

### THE THINKING TRIAD

---

### TYPES 5, 6, AND 7

Wisdom is not a product of schooling but of the
lifelong attempt to acquire it.

—ALBERT EINSTEIN, IN A LETTER TO JOSEPH DISPENTIERE

THE THINKING TRIAD, MADE UP OF FIVES, SIXES, AND SEVENS,
derives its power from the mind. Where the other triads find wisdom
in the gut and in emotional intelligence, the Thinking Triad's center
of strength and energy is the mind. These types are intellectual and

deeply curious, constantly taking in new information, synthesizing and cataloging it appropriately. The amount of pure knowledge a Thinking Triad type can retain is truly unbelievable to the rest of us.

The curse (and alright, the blessing too) of evolution is that as we've developed consciousness, we've also learned to strategize, to research, and even to plan. We are able to make predictions based on what we know, and document our fuck-ups for future generations. You're welcome, future kids!

People in the Thinking Triad not only are logical and knowledgeable but also tend to construct their lives around one common denominator: fear. They decided pretty early on in their lives that they were going to rely on, retreat to, and work out of their brains, using them as their primary source of both energy and comfort. The ancient memorization technique of the "mind palace" is a prime example of how Thinking Triad folks store up, catalog, and memorize information, both important and otherwise. The popular BBC series *Sherlock* highlights this in an entertaining, if heavy-handed sort of way, with Sherlock Holmes ordering folks out of the room so he can go to his "mind palace." It sounds goofy as hell, but honestly, it's not a bad way to describe some of our fear folks.

Let's talk about what the shit y'all are so afraid of! (Spoiler alert: it's super valid.)

The Thinking Triad feels unprepared to handle the world—like college freshmen who missed the first week of the semester and are now spending every class period trying to catch the fuck up. They have different ways of synthesizing the information they take in, but all three of these numbers have one basic response: MORE INFORMATION. Knowledge, they feel, is their key to both surviving and thriving. More articles, more interactions, and more experiences—they all add up to more information.

As in the other triads, one number is all "Gotta keep the world out," one number is all "Gotta keep myself out," and then one poor miserable little center number is concerned about the threats to their comfort zone posed by both the world and the self. It's a hard-knock life for Fives, Sixes, and Sevens. Let's talk about where fear plays out in each of the Thinking Triad numbers, and then, like, maybe muster up some hope for y'all as well?

## HOW FIVES FIT INTO THE THINKING TRIAD

Probably the first number that comes to mind when I say "Thinking Triad" is the Five, because these cuties (hi, date me, marry me) are the disembodied brains of the Enneagram, perfectly happy to go on taking in information forever and doing precious little about it. They're always in prep mode, like they're studying for an exam they're never actually going to take. Extra, extra, read all about it in the ENTIRE chapter I'm about to dedicate to these cute li'l suckers! The aforementioned Benedict Cumberbatch role as the titular Sherlock is like a Five on steroids. Architects and moody *Jane Eyre–*

**151**

style proprietors of intricate brain labyrinths, these cuties often read as mysterious to overanalyzers like me while inwardly feeling super incompetent and awkward about having to be a person all the time. Adorable. What can I say? I have a type.

If you can move through the world as a disembodied brain, taking up as little space as possible and minimizing other people's expectations of you, then it's easy to ignore the other centers of wisdom: your emotional center and your instinctive center. Your brain becomes your safe space, the place you retreat to, to recover from the life you're not really living and to stockpile the knowledge that you'll need to reenter the world someday—that is, if you ever really entered. Most Fives, being lowkey brilliant and having researched a few niche subjects enough to become the world's leading experts on them, eventually carve out a little space in the world for themselves, out of which they can disseminate useful information they've gathered and then promptly leave again at the end of the day. Fives have little or no faith in their ability to emote or relate properly, so they reluctantly navigate the world as people for a few hours daily and then Irish-goodbye the hell out of us when they're ready to retreat.

Fives are worried we'll find out that they missed the first week of the semester of life and that we'll punish them for it when we do. They tend to believe the only thing they can trust in the world is their own brain, and they're pretty sure even that is not prepared to take on the shit show that is life.

When Fives are at their healthiest they go to Eight, where they stop preparing and choose a course of action, convinced of their own competence. No one's going to give you a fucking certificate, boo. Nobody's going to tell you you're ready, because chances are you're not. Ready is a myth. Jump in. You're ready when your feet leave the diving board.

## HOW SIXES FIT INTO THE THINKING TRIAD

Sixes are also top-notch stockpilers, but their version of bunker brain usually leans toward the more pragmatic side of things. They're not just stocking up on abstract ideas; they're literally building a storm shelter around themselves. They're worried about their material well-being as well as that of everyone they love and even a lot of folks they only marginally give a shit about. If worrying could be an Olympic sport, Sixes would take the whole damn podium. Because they're so overrun by anxiety, they hustle to find an authority figure or belief system or ideological net that will hold them—something outside themselves they can trust. I've watched Sixes cling white-knuckled to boyfriends and religious systems that have long since failed them simply because admitting that the thing they were banking on failed them is a Six-ish nightmare.

As the root number in the Thinking Triad, the Six directs fear energy both outward, toward the world around them, and inward, at themselves—lucky them. Theirs is a constant battle between relying on outside systems and being suspicious of the very people and places they've learned to rely on. Sixes pull back, forge ahead, pull back, then forge ahead. Their longing for intimacy and their deep, abiding wariness of the very people they want to be intimate with is kind of a snake-eating-itself dilemma. A Six can call you in a frenzy to vulnerably tell you about whatever is fucking with them today and blame it on you in the same call!

Healthy Sixes integrate to Nine, where the bunker brain becomes a patio brain (just go with me here). Convinced that the wisdom others rely upon is good enough for them too, integrated Sixes take a deep breath and join the world, drinking deeply of the present and meeting each challenge with spunk, spirit, and, most of all, security—the kind that one can only give oneself.

## HOW SEVENS FIT INTO THE THINKING TRIAD

Sevens have the most fun of us all, but if you watch closely and long enough, there's a hint of frenzy to all the fun having that highlights how hard they're trying to stay ahead of themselves. Their worst nightmare is that their feelings will catch up with them. They've been running so long they're not even sure what they're running from anymore. They just know they gotta (1) get the fuck away and (2) drown that shit out. These jokers are the Oscar Wildes of the Enneagram, making us all jealous and judgy of their seemingly heedless hedonism.

Escapism is a fucking religion for these kids. I swear to lady-god, Sevens have little brain hamsters tirelessly running on wheels in their heads, keeping them moving and experiencing, never processing or feeling. While not every Seven is the class clown or the life of the party, most Sevens report a fever-brain phenomenon. Even when they lie down at night, their bodies exhausted from the exertions of the day, their minds are still hopped up and ready to take in more. While they're probably not the first personality type that comes to mind when you think of the word "fear," Sevens are experts at staying just a step ahead of it. I think of the 1992 Disney classic *Aladdin*, with Prince Ali hopping around the marketplace like it ain't no thing, staying one step ahead of the coppers while charming bitches. That song is the Seven anthem.

When Sevens are at their healthiest, they integrate to Five, choosing to go deep rather than wide. They realize that the greatest adventure is rooting deeply in the true self. They never lose their passion and curiosity for learning but instead find that focusing in on the people and things that give them abiding joy is more fulfilling than any emotional or experiential bender.

## ONCE UPON A TIME: A THINKING TRIAD ORIGIN STORY

Growing up is a hoax—pass it on! The child within is a real thing—tell your friends! It's wild how much the shit that affects us now can be traced back to our formative years. Children internalize basically everything. They watch all the stupid shit everyone pulls. Never forget that tiny humans are whole actual people inside those roly-poly little skin envelopes.

Riso and Hudson compare the Thinking Triad dilemma to the separation phase of toddlerhood, when the child starts to realize that they're actually an independent person from their mom or nurturing figure and decide they need to sally forth and make their own ill-advised and deeply foolhardy decisions (like walking, for example).

For the Thinking Triad, separation is a daily activity. Fives retreat from relationships and connection, feeling like they don't have what it takes to interact with people and feeling like close proximity to other humans kinda harshes their vibe. (Maybe your vibe needs to be harshed, babies—just a thought.) Sixes start obsessing about which systems and authority figures will make them feel safe but also independent, secure but free. Sevens keep themselves moving, trying on everything for size and settling on nothing.

All of these are separation stances—reactive, knee-jerk shit that keeps Thinking Triad numbers from realizing the full potential of their awesome-ass brains. In their quest for security and independence, all three types end up leaning on personality ledges, mucking around in the same fucking brain ruts for years on end, and actually, counterintuitively, fostering dependence in one way or another: Fives, on their own minds; Sixes, on whichever charismatic boss or cozy ideology is the flavor of the day; and Sevens, on whatever the next high is.

Riso and Hudson tell us that the strength of a Thinking Triad number is the miraculous opposite of their personality ledges: the "quiet mind."[1] The calm, competent, spacious mind is the gift that Fives, Sixes and Sevens bring to the table of human experience, but only when they've given it to themselves first. This requires a fuck-ton of bravery from each of them. Their survival stories have made them avoid the quiet mind in favor of hyperactivity, anxiety, and catastrophizing. It's part of the human condition that we believe there is always more to do—that doing, whether it be researching, worrying, or moving endlessly rather than just being, will help us arrive at the support we so desperately seek.

Truth is, kids, we need your brains. I don't think y'all realize how much we gut and heart folks depend on you. You're our teachers, our mentors, our oracles, and our ride-or-die bitches. We lean

---

1. Don Richard Riso and Russ Hudson, *The Wisdom of the Enneagram* (New York: Bantam, 1999).

on your foresight. We marvel at your knowledge. We soak in your love of learning, and we live for the ways that you synthesize creativity and active problem solving. You bridge our gaps.

We will need all of your research and ingenuity to assist us as we imagine better futures, stunt on injustice, and just generally cause meaningful mayhem. We will need you behind the scenes, putting the theological and political and ideological puzzles together for us, creating the framework out of which gut folks can act and heart types can feel.

Remember, though, that your deepest, dearest, and longest relationship is with you. You are the point of you, and I'll say it till I'm blue in the face. As we dig deeper into your types in the coming chapters, I challenge you to look yourself in the eye and ask what it is you really need from you. Your true self has been waiting your whole life to tell you.

# MILLENNEAGRAM
# 5

## THE DETECTIVE

"

Courage starts with showing up and
letting ourselves be seen.

**BRENÉ BROWN,** *DARING GREATLY*

"SO, HOW'S THE SEX LIFE GOING?" I ASKED MY CLOSE FRIEND Emily.

Okay, I did not ask it like that. The real question was much more inappropriate. I have no boundaries—it's whatever. You get the gist.

"Well . . ." she said excitedly, lowering her voice as if she was about to impart some juicy, dirty tidbit. I leaned in. I live for juicy, dirty tidbits.

"I had us fill out sex questionnaires with yes, no, and maybe about which stuff we want to try. Then I read through both of our responses, charted our overlaps, and put the results on a graph for us to compare!"

I stared incredulously at the monster before me, who had just found a way to quantify the intimate connection between her and her spouse. In that moment, there was nothing I wanted to do more than remove her brain from her skull and figure out what the fuck was going on up there. I refrained.

It occurred to me that this was actually a really life-giving way for my best friend to process new information about her sex life, and while there was nothing I understood less, I could let her have this one. Information gathering is how she makes sense of her world—whether it's choosing a political candidate, researching systemic injustice on Twitter, or jumping on some new fitness bandwagon. So, wisely and thoughtfully, I shouted and screeched and gave her an enormous amount of shit about it, which honestly is the only reasonable response to finding out your Person is a soulless Feelings Robot.

JK. But only mostly. I already knew she was one of those.

## TRUE DETECTIVES

Fives are thinkers and questioners. They see all of life as research, hanging back a bit from the stream of human experience to watch, reflect, and take some fucking notes. I call them the Detectives because for Fives, all of a life is a riddle to be solved. They're insatiable in their quest for knowledge, taking in and cataloging information at a rate you and I brain paupers can only dream of. Like cerebral astronauts, Fives seek to go where no mind has gone before—to test the limits of human experience and find everything there is to know at our edges.

Fives are concerned that maybe they're less equipped to function in the world than the rest of us, so gobbling down information is their coping mechanism in an effort to feel more prepared. Unfortunately, all too often, as their information banks grow, their insecurities do as well.

## BOMB-SHELTER BRAIN

When it comes to emotional engagement, less is more for a Five. They sense that their feelings reserves are lower than their counterparts, and they have to ration their connections. It's like they've created a bomb shelter they retreat into when they're stressed or overwhelmed. This bomb-shelter existence allows a Five to feel like they're in control, that their heart space is tidy and manageable. Independence to a Five is synonymous with nonintrusion: *You stay out of my way, and I'll stay out of yours. Don't need me, and I won't need you.*

And to a point, it works. People learn not to rely on Fives for the emotional engagement they rarely offer. Expectations are managed, and Fives get to slip back into their most comfortable position, removed from the whitewater stream of engagement: always observing and never diving.

It's all a bit miserly, though, isn't it? The impetus to withhold is what equates the Five with their chief passion of avarice, or stinginess, which essentially, within the bounds of the Enneagram, means emotional hoarding, which we'll get into more in the next section. The comfort zone for a Five is their headspace. Their heart, like an atrophied muscle, sort of shrinks back with minimal usage. A super cute metaphor, I know, but you get the idea.

When a Five does venture outside their comfort zone, it's often in service of "research." They want to understand where other people are coming from or what they're experiencing, because the consumption of knowledge is key.

David Hall, a psychologist and contributor to the *Enneagram Journal*, describes in an article for this publication the nine types of energy the individual Enneagram numbers focus on. Each energy is part of the absurd but delightful experience of being human, but each number has one they tend to gravitate toward. Fives exert most often the energy of pulling, bringing more into their headspace. Hall says that Fives have a distinctive sense of themselves: "I am, somehow, actually made of knowledge—it is part of the fabric of my being."[1]

For Fives, what they know defines who they are. Their deepest fear is not being competent or capable enough to navigate life, and so their solution is more information, ad infinitum. Hall warns that the pulling energy can become so strong in Fives that they actually pull themselves into their headspace and lose touch with their hearts and bodies.

Ultimately, the pulling energy is just one facet of the human digestive process—we reach out, we grasp on to, and we pull in. For our knowledge to be of any actual use to us, though, we have to cata-

---

1. David Hall, "Yielding, Pushing, Reaching, Grasping, and Pulling: How Our Type Expresses Itself Energetically," *Enneagram Journal* 6, no. 1 (July 2013), https://katytaylor.com/wp-content/uploads/2017/06/Yielding-Pushing-Reaching-Grasping-and-Pulling.pdf.

lyze it into movement, which is the Five's greatest adventure and also their greatest challenge.

## PASSION: STINGINESS

A pretty dependable Five mantra is this: *If you don't ask much of me, I won't ask much of you.* Fives try to pare down their needs so as to be less dependent on others while they "prepare" to rejoin the world. This also explains their core passion, stinginess, or avarice. They like to withhold and to distance themselves from others, because they just don't feel like they quite have the people skills to connect on a meaningful level most of the time. Frequently Fives complain about getting "peopled out," expressing a need to spend time away from the outside world after having exerted social energy in almost any capacity, be it in the workplace or blowing off steam with friends. This impulse is a little more intense than your average introvert vibe, because it's less of a simple recharging alone situation and more of an intentional withholding of energy thing.

The myth of scarcity is alive and well among Fives too—their grasping energy, trying to gather and stockpile resources for fear of running out, is much like the Six's bunker-brain situation. Because they see themselves as deficient in some way, ill-prepared to handle the tornado of human experience, Fives needs to believe they are knowledgeable experts in some way—or at least getting there.

## SURVIVAL STORY: SLEUTHING OUT THE WHY

When I was old enough to watch movies about kissing under the watchful eye of my mother and her fast-forward trigger finger, I watched the 1986 film *A Room with a View*, which struck me as a very strange film about a lot of strange people, but I was oddly mesmerized. The protagonist, Lucy Honeychurch, goes to Italy with her chaperone and runs into this golden-headed dandy, who happens to be a very withdrawn, fascinating sort of person and just happens to tag the art in innocent hotel rooms with great big graffiti "WHYS" for no apparent reason other than his being overwhelmed with that one singular question.

Why?

Fives are fixated on the why of a thing. A part of them—one that has been with them since they were very young—believes they are somehow less capable of approaching the mystery of life than others are, and as such, their need for research, for gathering and amassing information about themselves and the world around them, is never complete. "Why?" is the one question they cannot stop asking and the one question they will never fully answer.

Try telling *them* that, though.

We all get stuck in a rut of half-truth, a message that has helped us to survive thus far but has narrowed or obscured our vision at the same time. Our "personality," far from being an accurate depiction of our true self, is constructed of coping mechanisms and convenient

**166**

veneers that have written the script of our survival stories while, like benevolent captors, keeping us safely stored in cages of our own constructing. The half-truth that Fives fixate on at a very young age is that they are somehow less capable than their peers—that they are missing a key skill set that would enable them to move comfortably through the world. Reacting to this message, they retreat into their minds, amassing information like their life depends on it, because they're pretty sure it does.

When you approach life as a puzzle to be solved, a moment will arise when the pieces seem to fit, at least temporarily. All of your theories and perspectives, the circumstantial evidence you have gathered and cataloged, will seem to present to you a blueprint by which you can organize all incoming information. Riso and Hudson call this the "tinker toy" mentality,[2] and the behavior it elicits resembles the Six fixation on systems by which to order life. The systems that the Five relies on, though, are often more ideological than pragmatic and serve as a means of keeping true-self experience at a healthy arm's length. They're often cobbled together from a variety of influences and ideologues, and they highlight the Five's need to have a unique take on the world as it is. They worry that if their ideas aren't unique or cutting-edge enough, they didn't really delve as deeply as they could.

Answer is, yes, boo, you're overthinking it.[3]

---

2. Don Richard Riso and Russ Hudson, *The Wisdom of the Enneagram* (New York: Bantam, 1999).
3. Everything.

## WINGS

If a Five spent most of his life not doing a thing, you better fucking believe he's not about to start. (Unless it's for "research" purposes . . . basically just a cute Five excuse for doing a thing they want to do while not letting on how badly they want to do it.) Fives have very strong opinions about the shit they don't like, which is usually shit they haven't given a chance—but again, try telling them that. Their confidence in themselves, which often *reads* ironclad to the uninitiated, only extends as far as the activities and branches of knowledge they have extensively, obsessively researched and mastered.

A Five with a Four wing (the Tortured Artist) experiences a significant pull out of their mind by the Four wing, which tantalizes them with golden-goose promises of creativity and connection. But, being Fives and shit, they bring a lens of analysis to their relational engagement, keeping "in the moment" just out of reach. 5w4s are the kinda folks who will go out with every kind of person once, and then document the shit out of it. One dear Five friend of mine turned her dating experiences into a spreadsheet, noting what reactions she experienced to different sorts of dudes in order to, I imagine, arrive at the pinnacle of dating knowledgeability. For a Five, feelings are a thing to be solved rather than experienced. And therein lies the motherfuckin' rub.

When a Five is heavily influenced by the Four wing, they experience an overwhelming need for connection coupled with a knee-jerk reaction to withdraw in the face of discomfort or stress. They tend to espouse the romantic ideal that given enough different kinds of connections and interactions, they will happen upon someone who will be a game changer and will overcome their withdrawing urges once and for all. Of course, that's a helluva lot of pressure for any one friend or partner. The 5w4 may branch out, attempting to take on other romantic partners, or they may dramatically pull themselves out of the dating game entirely, expecting the game changer to find them if the 5w4 just speaks that person into existence. There's a sense that their eyes are too big for their stomachs relationally.

After a certain point, the 5w4's need for connection will give out, exhausted by the heart-space pull of the Four wing. This is to be expected and accepted! It might be due to work stress or an epiphany in therapy or just the general daily pressure of being exposed to someone. There might not be a "moment" at all. 5w4s will eventually retreat from the engagement they themselves have sought out, and those of us who love them will just have to deal. All relationships have ebbs and flows, and some numbers experience bigger waves than others. It's not something to shame yourself for, my 5w4 babes, but to be aware of. Notice without judgment. You're good at observing, after all! Isn't that, like, your hobby? So turn that shit around and observe the fuck outta yourself.

With the Six wing (the Oracle), however, the avarice of the Five is fortified by the anxiety of the Six. International humans of mystery, these ones. Less aware of how they are perceived by their peers, 5w6s read as even more cerebral, guarded, and often attractively mysterious. (Try to remember that they are in no way trying to be. It's all in your head—or perhaps, more accurately, it's all in THEIRS.)

Fives find that their incessant need for research and categorization plays quite nicely with their Six wing, which fills them with latent anxiety about their relationships, their present, and their future. The Six wing keeps them deeply and loyally entrenched in relationships that they open themselves up to, since the people they let into their lives are few and far between. But once you're in, there's really no way out. Emily calls herself a "prickly barnacle" because while she might keep you at arm's length a bit, she will never let you go either.

## INSTINCTUAL VARIANTS

### Self-Preserving Fives

The instinctual subtypes bring a little more color to the Five energy. The Self-Pres Five is entitled "Castle" by Beatrice Chestnut in her book *The Complete Enneagram*,[4] as if we needed more parallels to the Sherlock mind-palace shit. Just gonna keep beating that dead horse!

---

4. Beatrice Chestnut, *The Complete Enneagram: 27 Paths to Greater Self-Knowledge* (Berkeley, CA: She Writes Press, 2013), 32.

Self-Pres Fives, however, like to align their actual physical surroundings with their sanctuary or bunker brain, meaning they like to have an office, library, basement, or laboratory for retreating from the world and conducting their research away from the watchful, prying minds of, like, other people. Their physical boundaries are as important as their brain ones. Self-Pres Fives are the ones most likely to retreat from actual human relationships, intending and usually succeeding at not needing anyone.

## Social Fives

Social Fives create networks of other specialized experts in their fields—the relationships they create often look more like colleagues and partners than actual friends. They want to surround themselves with folks who align with their values, sorta gathering an echo chamber around them. This behavior reads like classic academic bullshit—you know, when people who know a lot sit around dryly discussing topics in terms that anyone outside their extremely specialized field will be hopelessly lost listening to? We've all been to that dinner party.

Social Fives tend to search for the ultimate answer to the "why" question, an ideology that can stand in for actual conviction and spirituality. While Social Fives may be fun as shit and better at conversation and visible engagement than other Fives, anyone with half a handle on their feels will be able to notice the tangible distance put in place by Social Fives, who are intent on not feeling things if at all humanly possible.

### Sexual Fives

A Sexual Five wants to find that one person who Gets It. They may have all the ordinary relational hang-ups as the other Fives, but they put a high price on finding an intimate connection with someone they can divulge all of their specialized thoughts to, someone who will be their intellectual match and sparring partner. These Fives are more overtly emotional than the other two subtypes, as their penchant for distance and withholding continually creates a vicious cycle, pushing Sexual Fives further away from the connection they seek.

What they fail to realize is that the more idealized their vision of the perfect partner becomes, the less likely they are to find this person among the land of the fucked-up living. Few can rise to that occasion for an extended period of time, and so the Sexual Five ends up feeling like they're Alone Forever and too difficult to love, simply because they made loving themselves an undoable task.

## BRAIN, MEET BODY: INTEGRATION AND DISINTEGRATION FOR THE FIVE

So the question is, my beautiful baby Five, how can you take all your know-how and catalyze it into right action? How can you peel your observer self off that personality ledge and step into the flow of your life? Remember that "safe" and "comfortable" are two different things.

Five goes to Eight in health, calling on all their meticulous research to assist them in charting their best lives now. The hemming and hawing comes to an end, and the Five embarks on a journey forward, fueled by and wielding their expertise as both a shield and a weapon.

Come down out of your head, boo. You got shit to teach us.

I know it feels wild and unpredictable out here. Maybe it feels like I'm stealing your sanctuary, your safe space, a bit, and you lowkey hate me. That's fine, honey. Everybody needs a scapegoat when they're afraid. Awareness can feel like torture, because, well, let's be real: life kinda sucks, and being present to it can feel like subjecting yourself to pain that is both cruel and unusual.

When it comes to unhealthy Fives, Riso and Hudson give it to y'all straight when they say that Fives "try to figure out how to live life without actually living it."[5] DAMN, the SHADE. Your self-image dictates that you separate from life, that you nurse an outsider complex and see yourself as different, as Other. This is a classic disintegrated Five because it's unhealthy to see yourself as a segmented, compartmentalized self.

---

5. Don Richard Riso and Russ Hudson, *The Wisdom of the Enneagram* (New York: Bantam, 1999).

Here's the deal, though, Fives: You ARE a whole person. You are not a disembodied brain. The knowledge that you have acquired has real, pragmatic uses in the world around you, and—news flash— you're way more fucking prepared than the rest of us. The rest of us are just out here flailing around, rushing headlong into shit we didn't think through and didn't see coming. Where you fear you're incompetent, you actually have a leg up on us. Time to use it. Are you waiting for someone to give you fucking permission? Is some heavenly being going to hire a skywriter to inform you clearly when you have learned enough? Hate to break it to you, boo, but that's not how any of this shit works.

## PLAYING WELL WITH OTHERS: RELATING TO A FIVE WHEN YOU AREN'T ONE

Loving a Five is a long con. I can't recommend it for the faint of heart. You'll be puzzled and delighted and pushed away more times than you'll be able to remember. Keep short accounts. Resentment has a long memory. Model presence for your Five, and slowly you may watch them start to follow suit—as long as you let them think it was their idea.

One of the lies Fives believe about themselves is that freeing themselves from attachment to any one person, place, or thing (guess

Fives hate *nouns*—who knew?) requires pulling back from the current of life in general. In fact, the opposite is true. The only cure for attachment is wholehearted engagement with the story of our lives, and sometimes Fives have to be coaxed out into it. Challenge them out into their world without pushing them into it.

The key to having a relationship of any kind with a Five is to take things one step at a time. Because they're thinkers, they're also overthinkers, so everything in your relationship will take light-years longer than you imagined it would and require more discussion. Just go with it. Their brains are struggling to compute reality—to hold it down, to examine it, to make sense of it. That's a lotta fucking work. Be patient with your Five, and as you grow closer, know that they probably aren't trying to be withholding anymore; they're doing the best they can with understanding the feelings they're so uncomfortable with.

Heart types, it can be especially hard to relate to a Five, when all you want to do is FEEL ALL THE FEELS, and they're out here acting like a straight-up robot. Take my Five bestie, Emily. I've learned that quiet nights of sitting next to her watching a movie, drinking our weight in wine, and not divulging our deepest, darkest secrets can be as important for our relationship as the wild vulnerability that tends to be more my style. But also, if you ever need to phone a friend, you better believe a Five is going to be the one you call.

## LAST CALL FOR FIVES

Attachment is, at its core, the lie that something outside of yourself can provide the security you seek, and you're right to avoid it, Fives. Pat yourselves on the shoulder and maybe dust off some chips while you're there. Engagement, on the other hand, means living in the stream of yourself, feeling your feelings, thinking your thoughts, speaking your mind, and creating your peace. You have to be present, and being present means you have to do some thinking on the fly.

What's funny is that this emotional stinginess you possess, this withholding of yourself, is in fact its own form of attachment. Don't guffaw at me. Just listen. You're clinging to a perception of yourself as isolated, as separate, as uniquely ill-built for connection, as running low on emotional funds. This is your myth of scarcity.

Isolation is a self-fulfilling prophecy, y'all. The more you believe it of yourself, the more you will implement it in your life. You'll hold old friends and new connections at arm's length, believing yourself incapable of providing the emotional labor necessary to grow in the intimacy you need. I'm not saying you gotta be an open book; I'm just saying you gotta let a few precious and carefully selected friends read you.

Recall that sharing knowledge is not the same as sharing YOUR-SELF. You Fives have a tendency to share what you believe as filler information for your actual feelings. I know it can be troubling when said feelings don't line up with your principles. Welcome to being a goddamn human person.

Your childhood wound dictates that you believe other people aren't trustworthy, and I'm gonna be a bad Enneagram person here and say, for the most part you're right. People are the worsssst. But to every rule there is an exception, and I'll be damned if some of those exceptions might not be sitting right under your very nose. Look around you and see who has stuck it out with you. Who listens to your random, very specialized rants that make you a horrible party guest? Who leans on your wisdom and respects your brainwork? Who makes space for you to be the goddamn nerd you were born to be? Keep those people. Prickly barnacle them right the fuck up.

When you start letting yourself feel things, the other pent-up shit you've been stuffing into your heart chest may come spilling out too. Old wounds, old rejections, old fears. I know it's hard, but feel all that shit. It will pass. Your body may go apeshit for a minute, unused to your presence. For most of your life you've been faking like you don't have needs, and your body has learned to adapt to the crumbs you throw her. Give her a minute to settle into your intentional kindness. Never forget that she's your first, oldest, and closest friend.

Baby Fives . . . never lose your curiosity. Never stop asking why. Someone's got to. Ask the questions that others are afraid to. Just remember that after the why, there is the what and the how of the rest of your life. Answer all your questions. Remember that the perspectives of others are as valid and valuable as your own, and use your curiosity to explore the depth and breadth of the human experience.

Live your life in real time. You have all the tools to slay this shit. You've got this. Nobody else will be able to convince you of that but yourself, so repeat it to yourself until you believe it.

Your knowledge is your power. When you allow it to bleed down into your heart and body, you'll find that you know instinctively how to move, what decisions to make, who to love, where to go, and what burdens to take on. It will require some bravery on your part to join us down here in the bustling, stressful, glorious dance that is life. Your feet will get stepped on a bit. You'll get jostled. Someone with two left feet might ask you to dance and throw you off your game for a while. It's okay. Experience is a good teacher too.

# MILLENNEAGRAM
# 6

## THE ORACLE

"

You have yet to learn how kind time is.
And life has something for you—I feel it.
Go forward and meet it fearlessly, dear.

**LUCY MAUD MONTGOMERY,**
*EMILY OF NEW MOON*

THE PHONE RANG, FIFTEEN MINUTES BEFORE OUR FRIEND date, like clockwork. I knew exactly who it was. With a giggle that was half a sigh, I picked up.

"OH HEY, BITCH." My extreme lack of surprise hung in the air.

"Hey," my friend Maria responded with a guilty laugh. "I just was . . . I just was calling to make sure we were still on."

"For the date we have in fifteen minutes," I said, clarifying, but just to give her grief.

"YES, OKAY. I just wanted you to know that I am leaving my house in about three minutes, and then the map is saying it will take twelve to get there, just so you know."

"So fifteen minutes, then," I said. "Like we originally planned."

"LISTEN, I JUST HAD TO MAKE SURE!" she shouted back at me in all caps. "It's okay if that time doesn't work for you," she quickly followed up.

"Oh my fuckin' god, YES. I will be there, okay? Calm yourself," I retorted, laughing.

This was a super-common occurrence in our longtime friend affair that had morphed into something more like siblings than polite friends. She was my best friend of fifteen years for a reason: typical of most Sixes, she is loyal as fuck and gives me an overwhelming outpouring of devotion and attention daily. I was used to the triple-checking of my dear anxious Six, a small price to pay for her incredibly devoted friendship.

## THE BIRTH OF AN ORACLE

In spite of their deep-seated anxieties, Sixes tend to hide their neuroses by being outgoing and upbeat. They read like the everyman of the Enneagram. Friendly, engaging, and encouraging on the outside, while inside they're cautious, anxious, suspicious, fearful, and faithful. As the center number of the Thinking Triad, the Six has never met a thing they couldn't overthink, and they tend to guard against perceived dangers both from the world outside and the world within. As a result, they're beset by fears.

I call the Six the Oracle because every Six I've ever loved has been so committed to imagining all possible scenarios—usually focusing on all the ways a thing could go wrong—that their precious catastrophizing little brains are always ready with invaluable advice. They're like fucking Doctor Strange, that kooky Marvel superhero with his hand on the pulse of time, who can close his eyes and consider millions of potential outcomes. If my longest and dearest friend Maria, a quintessential Six, tells me to jump, I fucking jump, y'all. Okay, alright, maybe not immediately, but eveeeentually I get around to following her advice.

While there are said to be more Sixes than any other number walking around in the world, they can look quite different from one another in demeanor and even in behavior. Anxiety brings out different reactions in all of us, and for Sixes, when given the choice between fight or flight, they're about evenly split down the middle. While all Sixes are fairly fixated on security and authority, and they make decisions based on their fear that no one is quite trustworthy, some Sixes (called phobic Sixes) react by keeping their heads down and following the status quo to the letter and some (called counterphobic Sixes) react by acting out against accepted norms. As Riso and Hudson say, "No matter what we say about Sixes, the opposite is often also as true."[1]

Sixes are ripe with possibility. Because they're constantly staring down the barrel of their own fear, being alive is kind of an adventure. Every day is an opportunity to test a comfort zone, confront a particular and specialized anxiety, or face a new dragon. There would be no David without a Goliath to face.

---

1. Don Richard Riso and Russ Hudson, *The Wisdom of the Enneagram* (New York: Bantam, 1999).

## PASSION: FEAR

When Sixes aren't operating from the foundation of their truest selves, capital *F* Fear takes over. It orders their motivations, controls their emotions, and guides their steps. When this happens, they're more likely to succumb to the inhuman demands of modern capitalism, to ignore the interests of others in favor of their own, to keep their heads down and stay small. Self-actualization is for the stupid.

Fear is a hella relatable human emotion. To some extent, we are all bound to it. Our sweet baby Sixes contend with fear in a unique way and embody what it means to search for a source of security—something to anchor them, to hold them down, to surround and root them.

What holds a Six back from presence is anxiety. All too often their fear of something outweighs the actual danger of the thing itself. This fear gets in the way of their being in each moment as their truest self. What a Six struggles—but needs—to understand is that things can go wrong, and they cannot always see it coming. The best way they can prepare for it is to connect to, to move and breathe out of, their true self.

Once a Six grasps being more present in themselves and with the world around them, they can start to heal the core wound within that tries to find a source of security. What we all eventually come to find sooner or later is that the source of our security can never be found outside ourselves. You had it within you, darling Six, all along. The call is coming from inside the house!

We've all experienced moments of fixation on particular negative possibilities, but catastrophizing is kind of business as usual for the Six—one of many reasons why even the loveliest Sixes report that living in their brain is fucking hell. As Riso and Hudson say, "Sixes tend to err on the side of caution."[2] Understatement of the century. Because hypothetical crises are always happening in the Six's brain, encountering real-life catastrophes is just a matter of course.

## SURVIVAL STORY: HUNG JURY

Sweet baby Sixes, perhaps there was someone in your past who was loving but erratic, a nurturing figure you depended on but did not find wholly dependable. Perhaps there was a reason to be always on your guard. Perhaps the environment that surrounded you, from which you felt unable to extricate yourself, was chaotic at best and menacing at worst. Early on, you internalized the message that someone in power over you, someone you probably loved, was not to be trusted. Could be God. Could be a parent. Either way, suspicion set in.

---

2. Riso and Hudson, *Wisdom of the Enneagram*.

Where other numbers may find themselves taking foundational relationships for granted, Sixes are never done questioning, cross-examining, interrogating. THE DEFENSE NEVER RESTS. This is also why a lot of people tend to be mistyped as a One when they are in fact a Six—the internal court is going on but for different reasons.

It's not even necessarily that your fave Six doesn't trust other people—it's that they don't trust their UNDERSTANDING of those people. There's always more to know, and Sixes will not rest until they do. Will they ever feel like they've arrived at enough information? That's another question entirely.

"If it ain't broke, don't fix it" is the Six's nemesis proverb. They're far more likely to live by something along the lines of "If it ain't broke, how can you be sure?" They're compulsive checkers, just-make-sure-ers, and how-do-you-know-ers. They build their emotional bomb shelters out of research and reassurance, and yet their stockpiles are never quite full. Gathering more skills to allay threats, Sixes often subtly self-sabotage their own plans by becoming lost in the weeds of securing their own perimeter.

We see an obsessive need to research in both Fives and Sixes, as they occupy adjoining spots in the Thinking Triad. However, like so many other instances in the Enneagram, all is not as it seems. We've got to look at motivation vs. behavior. While Fives are gathering information in order to feel more competent and capable, Sixes are gathering information to stave off the fucking apocalypse. One more internet rabbit trail and they might just succeed.

WINGS

As card-carrying members of the Thinking Triad, Sixes are thinkers, but instead of forging into parts unknown like Fives, the Detectives, they are preoccupied with understanding information inside established systems, like mathematics, science, etc. When a Six moves to a Five (6w5), they marry the information retention of the Five with their natural problem-solving skills. They tend to be on the more serious side of things, projecting a magnetic, calm preparedness that's like chicken noodle soup for this hot-mess soul. 6w5s rarely want to draw attention to themselves, preferring roles that keep them behind the curtain rather than in front of it. Healthy 6w5s, however, can rise to the occasion, using their patiently acquired expertise to stand up for the marginalized or disadvantaged. They aren't just gonna run their mouths, though. When they speak up, it's because they've done their fucking homework and they're bringing all the receipts to the table, honey.

Sixes with a Seven wing (6w7s), on the other hand, come across a lot more carefree and comedic thanks to the fact that a Seven, the Party, is so outgoing. 6w7s kinda shy away from heavier topics in conversation until they know that you're somebody they wanna open up to. They bring a lot of the Seven energy to their interactions, and they hold on to family, friends, and responsibilities with a fierce and unyielding loyalty. These kids got jokes, often deflecting the impact of their fears and anxieties by making fun of themselves. When they're less healthy, 6w7s are less likely to ask for, let alone admit to themselves their need for, help.

One 6w7 slid into my DMs to tell me that on a very spontaneous Seven-ish whim she booked a last-minute ticket to Iceland, all psyched up for an adventure, and by the time she got there, she had so poisoned herself with stress that she couldn't sleep, got sick, and had to go to an Icelandic emergency room. That Seven wing will getcha.

## INSTINCTUAL VARIANTS

### Self-Preserving Sixes

"Self-Preserving Sixes" is such an oxymoron, one could almost call them "Six Sixes." If hypervigilance were a person, it would be a Self-Pres Six. These subtypes are quick to audit and test their closest relationships. Convinced they are always teetering on the edge of disaster, they will often pile their panic onto the nearest person, as if to say, "Fix this, please."

Self-Pres Sixes need to feel warm and surrounded; they want everywhere they go to feel like home, so they don't venture out of their immediate circle much, except for those counterphobic moments when they worry that their current strategy may not be working. Self-Pres Sixes are the security guards of their own lives, protecting the barrier, and making everybody check in and show their identification when they walk through the door—then suspiciously watching them until they leave.

## Social Sixes

Social Sixes have sort of a deceptive name, as they lean more on abstract ideologies to keep them afloat. They like authority, but they also like choosing who is the best authority—who deserves their time and trust. Less warm than Self-Pres Sixes, Social Sixes are concerned with the role they play in their community, the rules they're meant to follow, and the standards they need to uphold.

Where Self-Pres Sixes are constantly questioning, Social Sixes manifest as being TOO sure about life. They know that once they start asking questions—once they start reexamining—they will never be able to stop, so they avoid it like the fucking plague. Along with average Ones, Social Sixes like to follow the rules, to present as *correct*. But while Ones adhere to their standards because they're guided by a deep intuition, Social Sixes are deeply concerned about getting in trouble with the powers that be.

This is where the whole God card can come into play super hard, because harmful and abusive views of God are exacerbated by the Six's anxiety brain. It's true for all the Six subtypes, to some extent, but whatever deity a Social Six is taught to believe in at a young age is the one they will continue to try to please throughout their lives, even when they stop technically believing in this deity. There remains still a nagging fear that he's watching and disapproving.

## Sexual Sixes

Sexual Sixes are the most obviously counterphobic of the subtypes, believing, according to Chestnut, that "the best defense is a good offense."[3] They charge toward the things that scare them, preferring to confront them head-on than kowtow or avoid them. What they do avoid, however, is expressing that they're afraid in the first place. Admitting it might make it real.

These folks often like to build up actual physical strength, to meet life more efficiently—getting jacked in the gym seems to them like a healthy coping mechanism to meet whatever life has to offer. They quietly mutter "Do your worst" to the world. These Sixes stifle their nagging doubts with self-assertion and even aggression, and can almost look like Eights from time to time with the bold-faced offensive front they launch against the objects of their fear.

All Sixes are fixated on finding a framework, a system around which they can organize their present, semi-accurately predict their future, and understand their past. Sixes oftentimes were raised

---

3. Beatrice Chestnut, *The Complete Enneagram: 27 Paths to Greater Self-Knowledge* (Berkeley, CA: She Writes Press, 2013), 32.

with a particular set of beliefs that, as formative and impressionable kids, they entangled themselves around. Others reached adulthood and created their own set of beliefs. Regardless, there's a solid chance that you'll have to pry that cherished framework out of their COLD DEAD FINGERS, or make it seem like it was their idea to ditch it.

## AFTER THE STORM: INTEGRATION AND DISINTEGRATION FOR A SIX

Because anxiety is such a core concern for Sixes, integration to Nine is almost always a healthy journey for them. They learn to trust their instincts and, according to Riso and Hudson, become "grounded in their bodies."[4] Instead of floating around in the hypothetical future that may or may not ever happen, integrated Sixes learn to enjoy the here and now. Not to quote Kanye, but your presence is a present, bitch! Gift it to yourself!

Maria, who you met at the beginning of this chapter, fucking wins at that shit. An intense and counterphobic Six, Maria meets the everyday adventures of being a young mom with a sense of humor and an easy, messy grace. It took her a minute to get here, mind

---

4. Riso and Hudson, *Wisdom of the Enneagram.*

you. There was a fair bit of disintegration involved in the process of learning to see life as it actually is, rather than how her Six-y fever brain projected it would be or how her conservative Christian friends and followers expected it to be. Where she formerly would have tried to keep up appearances on social media, portraying to the world an idyllic view of domestic bliss, she now documents all the little joys and trials that come with having a curious, rambunctious mini-me running around. She delights in the little moments of peace and discovery that make up her and her son's lives. She believes in the magic of the mundane, and, damn girl, it shows.

So what's the flip side? A vague, unsettled feeling accompanies disintegrating Sixes as they start to realize that the system around which they have wound themselves lowkey sucks. Usually the knee-jerk reaction is a coping mechanism stolen from unhealthy Three: if they can't convince themselves they're happy and secure, then they damn well better convince you. When Six goes to Three, we see endless syrupy Instagram posts about how GrEaT everything definitely is, how happy they definitely are, and how calm and content they are definitely feeling on the inside.

Whenever you see a rising percentage of these obnoxiously perfect posts from your BB Six, you can pretty safely assume that all is not well. But as we've seen in the other types, disintegration is not a bad thing. It's a warning that can give us the information we need to redirect our lives toward wholeness. For Sixes, this means paying attention to when you feel the need to perform okayness. Who are you trying to convince that everything is fine? The answer is usually yourself.

## PLAYING WELL WITH OTHERS: RELATING TO A SIX WHEN YOU AREN'T ONE

As friends, Sixes are often giving, affirming, fun, and thoughtful—engaged, but not clingy. They're committed but concerned; happy, if a bit high-strung. The type has been dubbed the Loyalist because anxious Sixes feed the people who make them feel secure, and once they've adopted you, they're in it for the long haul. They'll weather your storms faithfully. They can be questioning ("Are we okay?") but rarely combative. It's like, *Awww, they were thinking about me.* So go get yourself a Six friend, ya hear? You'll never experience a more devoted and reliable oracle—someone who will peer into the muck of your life, foresee your disasters, and let you know what icebergs lie ahead.

When it comes to parents and partners, though, we see different patterns emerge. Enter the Interrogator.

As partners, Sixes want to feel dependent on you while acting independently of you. Rude, I know. The push and pull of loving a Six can be overwhelming for some. Sixes want to feel safe but not stifled, supported but not surrounded. Striking such a balance is hard for someone who doesn't actually take up residence in the Six's head, primarily because not even your Six could chart that balance for you. They know what they don't like but often have difficulty describing what they DO.

One time I asked Maria what made her pick her partner—how she chose one person to build a home and a future with. She said simply, "He felt like home." While this exceptionally romantic line could (and should) be inserted into next year's Hallmark Christmas rom-com, I think there's more to it than meets the eye.

Sixes need someone who will give them minimal reason to stress, someone who will need them without asking too much and feed their spirit without stuffing them. They need a home—just enough room, but not too much. Somewhere with windows and a big backyard. Someone they can both run away from and come back home to.

Just because a Six picks you, though, doesn't mean they're settled. All their behavior may suggest that they are. They may have designed the perfect living space or planned the next decade around your collective plans—hell, they may be having your babies. The constant fear of having the rug pulled out from under you kinda fucks with intimacy, though, and you may find your Six emotionally pulling away or scaring up problems just when the going gets good. Peace isn't a feeling a Six will trust easily. It takes bravery to accept happiness when it arrives, but they're equal to the task. Remind them.

## READY IS THE WRONG WORD

All right, Sixes. So here's the deal. Y'all are without doubt my favorite humans, and you can quote me on that. The other numbers will just have to deal. But here's what I need you not to do:

You don't have to catastrophize, sweet Six. Half the horrible shit you dream up is never going to happen, and the stuff that does will not be the stuff that you so carefully plan ahead for.

You don't have to push people away just to make sure they'll come back to you. Because one day you might accidentally push away the good eggs.

You don't have to force a feeling of belonging just to belong somewhere. There is no place, no system, no congregation, and no space that can provide for you what true self-love can.

Instead of forgetting all the times you WON at life, remember them. Write that shit down if you need to. Put a big garish glittery frame around that list of joys and accomplishments, and look at it whenever you need to remember who you are and what you can do.

Pause.

Sit.

Look around you.

Odds are, you have created a good thing.

Recognize your power, boo! Marinate in it. The wheels of anxiety will try to keep you grinding forward, but let me let you in on a little secret: there's no destination at the end of that road. That anxiety will never let up. You have to put your foot on the brakes and stop that shit. Get out of the car. Breathe some outside air. All you have is right fucking now, you hear me?

There is no such thing as perfect security. You will never find it. You will never get there. No matter how many times you talk shit out, to yourself or someone else, no matter how wholeheartedly you cling to this house or that family structure or this church or that friend group, you will not be able to hold all the pieces together. That's a surefire fail, pal. And frankly, it's a pretty boring way to live. Let go.

Try something new on for size. Everything you currently like is not everything you're going to like your whole life, okay? Sure, trying new shit is uncomfortable, but it's the pathway to pleasure. To wonder. To delight. And chances are, better orgasms too. You're literally boring *yourself,* 'kay?

Perhaps the biggest, deepest, widest lie you've bought, baby Six, is that it's possible to be completely prepared. Life is out here just slinging curveballs at you, and yet you have convinced yourself that, given enough research and anxiety, one day you'll be able to preempt them. But that's not how it works. You have to embark on life, even if you get hurt along the way. There's no such thing as ready.

Nobody is ready for trauma or hurricanes or car accidents or lay-offs. Nobody is really ready for love. The horrifying miracle of being alive is that nothing is a sure thing. The only part of our stories that we get to write are our reactions to our circumstances, what we make of the hands we are dealt, and which diving boards we choose to jump off of.

So jump, darlin', and start swimming. You've got this.

# MILLENNEAGRAM

## THE PARTY

**"**

Now, the party don't start till I walk in . . .

**KESHA ROSE SEBERT,**

**"TIK TOK"**

IT WAS MY FIRST NIGHT IN NASHVILLE AND MY FIRST NIGHT with my new roomie, Annie. My dad had just helped me drive across the country with what few belongings I owned in the back of my beige Toyota Corolla, and when he and I walked into my new place, angsty and travel weary, Annie was warming up yesterday's coffee in a skillet on the stove, bedecked in last night's eye glitter and a ripped black T-shirt that was torn so artistically you could almost believe it came like that.

I was instantly in love.

She piled me and my dad and Emily—our third and final addition to the iconic roomie trio that would come to be known by the sparkling moniker Velvet Hustle—into her old beat-up Expedition and took us out on the town. She had been in town for only a pair of weeks, but already she knew exactly how and where to show us a good time. Downtown parking was tricky, though, and I anxiety-squinted as we barreled around the impossible corners of a parking garage. Somehow we survived the ascent, and as we hopped out, Annie locked arms with me and paraded me down the street to what would become our favorite bar. We ate barbecue and fried pickles by the pound, shouting plans for the apartment over live music, and suddenly five hours had passed and it was time to go scare up some sleeping arrangements in our all but empty new home.

As we descended out of the parking garage, something felt off. As Annie navigated her big ole beast of an SUV around its corners deftly and confidently, Emily halfway shouted, "Shit, Annie, you're going DOWN the ENTRANCE!" My dad's eyes were smiling, but his fingers were gripping the armrests with a strength that gave his stress away.

Annie just laughed. No pause. No hesitation.

"What are you going to DO?" Emily asked.

"Well . . ." Annie paused, for a moment. "I guess I'm gonna trust the Lord and use my horn!"

And so, screeching with laughter and fear, I survived my first night with my favorite Seven. I would never be quite safe or quite the same again.

## AIN'T NO PARTY LIKE A SEVEN PARTY

I once punctuated a poem about a Seven I was into with the recurring line "You are so big."

While I'm hardly about to win any awards for my inspired verse, Sevens are the fucking Legends of the Enneagram, no mistake. They are larger than life. Front men. A total party. They are louder and livelier and more magnetic than any other number, and they won't let you forget it either. Whether they opt for the class clown route or the artistic visionary, Sevens are magnetically drawn to center stage. If you try to play keep-up with a Seven, you'll find their energy almost unparalleled. You won't match them, so quit trying, and don't wish you could. Burning bright and burning out is both an exciting and an exhausting way to live.

Sevens want to taste everything, try everything, experience everything. They consume activity and experience the way Fives consume knowledge. They're professional hobbyists, dabblers. They're walking parties, and they'll earn their name every day of the goddamn week.

Sevens are found in the Thinking Triad, which may come as a surprise based on how little thinking they *seem* to do. This triad is also the fear triad, though, and while Fives fear what's outside them, Sevens are afraid of what's inside. The trouble is that without a stable understanding of who they are and what the fuck they're about, forward motion for a Seven is going to be a constant start and stop. Everyone needs emotional fuel in their life tank, and a Seven who isn't integrated can find it only in spurts.

David Hall describes the "gift" of type Seven as the "head version of reaching . . . a questing, curious, adventurous probing into the unknown and undiscovered field of possibility."[1] Sevens imagine

---

1. David Hall, "Yielding, Pushing, Reaching, Grasping, and Pulling: How Our Type Expresses Itself Energetically," *Enneagram Journal* 6, no. 1 (July 2013).

the possible before anyone else can. They reach with their minds the way Twos reach with their hearts. The pure energy of reaching—a definitive feature of the human experience—can be admired most obviously in a Seven's wide-eyed wonder at the world that is, and the world that could be.

A Seven can do anything they set their minds to, and with apparent ease. Beginner's luck follows these fuckers the way awkward moments stalk the rest of us. If a Seven was ever to take advantage of this charmed coincidence and dig in deep on one of their newly discovered skills, well . . . it would be over for you hos. Good news for the haters is that the discipline required to do so is rarely there.

Good news for the Sevens is . . . that would be one hell of an adventure.

## PASSION: FOMO

The passion of the Enneagram Seven is "gluttony," which has little to do with food and a lot to do with consumption. Let's call it FOMO instead: the fear of missing out—of not getting enough. Natural hedonists and pleasure-seekers, the *what* that a Seven seeks is less important than the *how much* of that thing they seek. Sevens are masters of new experiences, adventure seekers and adventure creators, and life seems to naturally bring all of its wildest pleasures and curiosities to a Seven's door, as if by sheer magnetism. I encourage you to delve into the descriptions that Riso and Hudson provide in my absolute BIBLE *The Wisdom of the Enneagram* or Beatrice Chestnut's *The Complete Enneagram: 27 Paths to Greater Self-Knowledge*, which is literally all about this shit. I mean, 27 paths? She digs in deep, y'all. Get your interest piqued with my summary, and then go read the actual academic work you prolly should have started with, but here we fucking are. (*Winky face.*)

## SURVIVAL STORY: COMEBACK KID

Sevens are the Enneagram's resident comeback kid, and in the words of Christian-adjacent R&B recording artist Stacie Orrico, in her 2002 hit single, they sure know how to "bounce, bounce back." (I'm sorry, guys. I don't know *actual* pop culture references—my b.) More than perhaps any other type, Sevens know how to come back swinging after a breakup, a career dead end, or virtually any other setback that presents itself. Setbacks are often steamrolled instead of processed. As a jack-of-all-trades, a Seven possesses an uncanny knack for landing on their feet, like a cat spending extra lives. Processing loss is for other people—people with fewer options. Sevens are ready and raring to go with plans B, C, and D from the moment disaster strikes.

A lot of Sevens grew up in households or situations where avoidance seemed like the best self-protection move. If you don't think about the tough shit, did it really happen? Instead of facing problems, crises, or conflicts head on, Sevens realized they could skirt the problem and get the fuck out of the way just in the nick of time.

The trouble here is, just like emotional buildup, crises and calamities can't be hurdled over or outrun. This isn't a fucking steeplechase, y'all! The only way out is through, my li'l Seven honey, and in your hurry to get past the negative and the painful, you're really just allowing yourself to be shackled to an invisible anchor that will drag behind you wherever you go.

As scary as this may sound, lugging all that dead, unprocessed weight is what's actually holding you back from experiencing your biggest, wholest present and realizing your full potential. You wanna dream big? Cut that shit loose, babe.

Of course, to cut it loose you first have to face it.

Now, let's touch on the other half of the Seven survival story: the visionary vortex. Most Sevens I know are essentially stuck in a Bermuda Triangle of creation—too many ideas and too little follow-through. Their feet can't keep up with their damn brains . . . and usually no one else's can either.

It can be difficult to know, as a friend or co-conspirator of a Seven, exactly which idea to help them settle on. You want to feed off their passion and enthusiasm, and honestly, when you're sitting right in the stream of it, that shit will get you high.

It can be confusing to find out how little thought your fave Seven puts into the thing they actively love. They have a habit of barreling through life from social event to date to boyfriend's cousin's graduation party without a breath, and the weird thing is . . . they don't seem to need any of it. You can spot the moment when they wake from this fever dream—the moment we all have waking up from a hangover and trying to piece together the night before. *Where the fuck have I been? What have I even been doing? Time to focus.* A Seven's idea of "focus" swings them entirely to the other side of the pendulum: they lock themselves away in their rooms or offices or creative spaces, free from supposed "distraction." Unfortunately, the distraction is often coming from inside themselves, and it isn't the sort of noise that hermitting up can silence for them. The white noise they're trying to eradicate from their lives may be coming from their own brains, and no amount of shutting the world out will quiet it down.

The key truth that a lot of my beloved bb Sevens miss entirely is that action doesn't always translate as forward motion.

## WINGS

Sevens have a Six wing (the Oracle) and an Eight wing (the Dragon). Life seems to come easily to 7w6s—they're the quintessential optimists of the Enneagram, believing that life is good and meant to be enjoyed. They sort of breeze their way through, entertaining the fuck out of friends and coworkers and having beginner's luck at pretty much everything they try. They're a bit more all over the place than 7w8s—while both wings tend to weave big dreams and tire of them quickly, the Six wing keeps a Seven in line with a subconscious thread of anxiety. *On to the next!* When they're less healthy, there's a sense that they have to stay hyped, almost like they fear calm. 7w6s will try anything once . . . except introspection.

Thanks to the more focused and powerful energy of the Eight wing, 7w8s are more strategic and calculated than their easy-breezy counterparts. They want to try everything, and they are big dream weavers, but they tend to have more timely success when it comes to accomplishing the shit they set their sights on. 7w8s are often entrepreneurs with multiple side hustles, coming up with new visions before the previous ones are quite complete—sometimes before they're even begun.

## INSTINCTUAL VARIANTS

### Self-Preserving Sevens

Without the integration process enacted, all Sevens lean toward some semblance of excess. Self-Pres Sevens are less concerned with amassing things than they are with amassing people and stimulating experiences. Charmers and strategists, they are committed to generating the resources they need to not only survive but thrive.

They're earthy, sensuous, and hedonistic as well as scrappy and self-possessed.

## Social Sevens

Social Sevens are more obviously altruistic. They lean on their idealism to create an atmosphere of what Chestnut calls "counter-gluttony,"[2] a term I love because it describes the behavior while illuminating the fact that the do-gooding is wrapped up in subconscious self-interest. Ever the visionaries, Sevens imagine a world without pain, and then throw themselves headlong into attaining that vision, often with less strategy and more unmeasured self-sacrifice. The joy and wonder of the Seven is present, but it's often spent on helping people—not like Twos, for the approval of the Other, but to counteract the "selfishness" the Social Seven feels about meeting their own needs. (Both can be done—hi, balance—but we'll get there.)

## Sexual Sevens

Sexual Sevens are in love with the world. They are in love with everything that is good and beautiful and free of complication and pain—which, of course, in the fucked-up place we live in is not easy to come by, so Sexual Sevens fashion their own set of lenses with which to look at the world. Happiness is a helluva drug, and

---

2. Beatrice Chestnut, *The Complete Enneagram: 27 Paths to Greater Self-Knowledge* (Berkeley, CA: She Writes Press, 2013).

Sexual Sevens are afraid they'll run out if confronted with life as it actually is.

Sexual Sevens experience any kind of enthusiasm as contagious and the world as a smorgasbord of fun they must partake of. All three of these subtypes your fave Seven probably floats in and out of, but there's usually one point of focus, one attitude they will revert to most easily and often.

## DOWN BUT NOT OUT: INTEGRATION AND DISINTEGRATION FOR THE SEVEN

I am of the firm belief that every number on the Enneagram must come to a crossroads of sorts. Perhaps it's a storm of epic proportions; perhaps it's a gentle surrender. Like Cheryl Strayed says, "Acceptance is a small, quiet room."[3] Now, you'll have to keep this between us (I'd hate for the other numbers to get their panties in a wad—those Fours are so freaking *sensitive* and all), but integrated Sevens are my fave sorts of folks, and I'll tell you why.

An integrated Seven is possibly the most delightful sort of human. Sevens head toward Five in security and, in so doing, learn how to go deep instead of wide, how to zone in instead of zone out.

---

3. Cheryl Strayed, *Tiny Beautiful Things: Advice on Love and Life from Dear Sugar* (New York: Vintage, 2012), 352.

All of the wonder is still there, but it's DIRECTED. It's guided. They learn to pour all of that vivacious energy into the talents and endeavors that arrest them, that fascinate and inspire and hold them captive. We see all the expertise of the Five with none of the hubris—they approach research from a place of fascination. Integrated Sevens are genuinely fascinated with learning, with taking in and understanding the intricacies of the world, both its sunshine and its shadows, and using this information to fashion better futures.

A disintegrating Seven in crisis, however, will suddenly be reminded that in order to accomplish shit, they're gonna have to settle down and focus on one thing for a minute. When Seven disintegrates to One, they tend to try to limit themselves, setting precise schedules, holing up in their rooms until they complete X, and just generally trying to rein themselves in. Playing hard-ass with themselves can get them only so far, though, if their curiosity isn't piqued. Ya gotta keep a Seven guessing.

Disintegration to One can be useful for alerting a Seven to the fact that they're putzing around and not actually accomplishing any of their big-ass dreams. It's sort of a *Wait—where the fuck am I?* moment. It doesn't do to stay there, though, which is why integration to Five is such a crucial and delightful move for a Seven.

Another internet friend described the moment when her Seven fiancé decided to settle down and go all in on their relationship— when she realized that a relationship in itself can be an unending adventure. You can't project the course of love or chart your discoveries

**211**

in advance. You just have to jump into its changeful, exhilarating stream. When Sevens realize that going deep on something they care about can be just as fascinating as going wide, that's the sweet spot right there.

## PLAYING WELL WITH OTHERS: RELATING TO A SEVEN WHEN YOU AREN'T ONE

You might hit the neighborhood bar (or, better yet, a new one) every day of the damn week with a Seven and still run into the same emotional barrier every time—sort of a subconscious reminder on the part of the Seven that "hey, we're all having fun here. Let's not ruin it by bringing FEELINGS into this!" You'll know all their stories, yes. Interests, definitely. But hardcore emotional information? Less likely. If you can get a Seven drunk enough (which I'm not *recommending* per se), you may get a beautiful, articulate, tearful anecdote that gives you a window of insight into what goes on deep beneath the surface. That light-bulb moment is addictive, lemme tell you. You'll spend months, years even, trying to re-create that moment. Maybe the stars will align for you. Maybe they won't.

The thing is, you can't straight-up ask a Seven to self-disclose to you. Ya gotta coax that shit out of them. There are two strategies here: either be compelling and fascinating enough to get the Seven to engage with the experience of talking to you or be quiet and engaged enough for the Seven to see you as a willing audience.

You may feel the need to perform in order to regain or retain your Seven's attention, to become shiny in order to be noticed. Don't. Sevens are fucking allergic to clingy. There's often a sense, in conversation with a Seven, of them effectively looking through you until they decide that this conversation in front of them is the one that needs to happen right now—and then they're mesmerized. They're either going to whole-ass or no-ass a convo with you. Unfortunately, the anticipation of the next "moment," the next emotional high, can become addicting to an average Seven. Recognizing this pattern and rejecting the urge to (a) give the Seven what they want or (b) confront the Seven about their lack of presence is key.

You're not gonna convince a Seven to connect with you. I'm just gonna tell you that right now. It has to be their idea, or at least you gotta make them think it was. I'm not saying trap them, but I *am* saying build it and (maybe) they will come. Lay a foundation of calm, balance, active listening, and CHILLNESS. (Again, the whole allergic-to-expectations thing.) Patience and persistence are key, even if it takes years before your Seven realizes that's what they've been getting from you this whole time. It's a long con, but they're bound to facilitate so many treasured memories on your way there that I promise it's worth it.

## ADOPTING YOURSELF

All right, Sevens, I love y'all, but we've reached the ass-kicking portion of your chapter, and I'm not gonna hold back. Kisses. Let's get into it.

Your pure, expansive, unadulterated reaching energy is a fixture of your glorious existence. While most of us live our lives second-guessing as a coping mechanism, you Sevens somehow have managed to hold on to some of that childhood fairy dust of reaching toward everything around you like actual fucking Peter Pan. You've chosen to stay open to all things, which is a gift few of us can claim. The problem is that you're always reaching and not always holding on to anything in particular. Keep reaching, but it's up to you to decide what to grasp. To choose that effectively, you need to plant your feet firmly in the now and face yourself in all your vibrant, disappointing, human glory. Ya gotta have somewhere to grow from, and to grow from somewhere, you have to learn how to be here first.

To be now. To revel in the glorious confusion that is your life *today*. You're not promised another one.

I'm not asking you to be someone different than yourself.

I'm asking you to be you, here. Now.

You cannot grow without growing pains. I know that staying one step ahead of suffering is a full-time fucking job, and, girl, you've done your time. Avoidance is treading water hoping it'll get you somewhere. Knock that shit off. Outrunning yourself is not keeping you safe.

Maybe something happened a long time ago that made you feel unsafe in the first place. Maybe someone important was detached or felt dangerous—like someone you couldn't take on directly as a new little person, someone you had to look at sideways or maybe dance around. Maybe somebody important made you some promises they couldn't keep, or they could and they didn't. I'm really sorry about that, and it's not okay. Don't let anybody tell you that you should just be *over it* already or some tough-it-out bullshit like that.

What I will say is that nobody is gonna heal you but you.

You're the person who has to keep you safe. You're your own parent now, and part of being a good parent to yourself is having a standing shoulder to cry on available. Get it all out, honey. Ugly cry if you have to. Processing your pain is the only way to *not* get trapped in it. Avoiding it is actually keeping you stuck. I know, a mind fuck, right?

I believe in you. I believe in this. I believe in the inherent magic of your existence. I believe it is your power, your currency, and all I want is for you to spend it on purpose. Sparingly. Meaningfully. Don't let anyone siphon your power out of you, even if that person is you.

Listen to me, darlin'. I expect you to wonder.

I expect you to arrest us with the magnitude of your wonder.

I want you to teach us to reach again, to stretch out our hands without knowing what our fingers will find. It's the purest sort of faith.

I expect you to dream, big and wide and outrageous. I expect you to turn around and make those dreams come true yourself.

Yours will not be a linear path. You will often take two steps forward and three hundred back. Just remember that the backward steps do not erase or negate the forward: you are setting an intention and finding a rhythm.

The world
will move
with you.

I'M A
MILLENNEAGRAM
SEVEN, AND

**THE PARTY
HAS ARRIVED!**

# MILLENNEAGRAM GROUP HUDDLE

The Truth must dazzle gradually
Or every man be blind.

—EMILY DICKINSON,
"TELL ALL THE TRUTH BUT TELL IT SLANT"

Dearly beloved, we have gathered together
Today
To grow.

Growing is hard. The Enneagram makes that painfully obvious. But it's worth it—I promise.

You are being issued an invitation today. An opportunity to give up on the myth of scarcity that has fueled your survival story thus far. You are not too much, and you are not too little. You are fucking Goldilocks's dream porridge bowl. You are just enough. No one will give you permission to believe this about yourself. You will have to reach out and claim that shit.

When I was a kid, whenever I felt unmotivated or bummed, I would ask my mom, "Hey, can I get a pep talk about this?" Learning how to ride a bike? Pep talk. Finishing my seventy-five-book reading list for the seventh grade? Pep talk. Life is exhausting, and also it sometimes blows. Motivation is our most expensive and most crucial currency, and in order to motivate ourselves effectively, we have to understand how the fuck our brain works, why the fuck it works that way, and what fucking direction to even head in. So this right here is our Millenneagram group huddle—the part where I give you the most bomb-ass, drop-the-mic, Denzel-in-*Remember-the-Titans* pep talk, and you just have to sit there and get inspired. Get comfortable. Slouch. Manspread. Pour a mimosa. Settle in.

After all this digging into our innermost selves, I guess the question that we come to is: What is the fucking point in trying to change? After all, our survival stories have gotten us this far. Our brain ruts might be problematic, but, hell, we're still here, right? "Hannah," you say, "I'm kinda just cozy over here in my lil mud puddle. Why can't you just let me be lovable garbage?"

Now, you listen here to your Millenneagram mom.

You don't have to be perfect. Your teachers and your parents and your family and your culture have been requiring that nonsense of you for a long-ass time, and I'm not here to perpetuate that. You don't have to reinvent yourself, and you don't have to pretend you don't have some garbage parts of yourself that will probably always irritate you and others. What I AM asking you to do is fucking recycle yourself.

Don't allow yourself to add to the rapidly accumulating waste of humanity: I'm talking about the junkyard heaps of humans who challenge themselves little, ask themselves few questions, reveal their true selves to no one, and spend their lives being just okay. We can't all be summer-camp high all the time. But I want to rest knowing that, when push comes to shove, when love comes to light, when bullshit comes knocking, you will be ready to meet it.

Each of us has the capacity for great love, big dreams, and right action. We may be glorified monkeys with anxiety, but it's because we fucking give a shit. Unfortunately, but understandably, we've convinced ourselves that our fears and our traumas should write out our survival stories. We've spent our lives trying to prove to ourselves that our ego fixations are who we really are, that we don't really care about or need anyone, that we're content with just "all right."

I'm here to say: girl, bullshit.

Life is always better when we have a mantra we can tell ourselves instead of the lies and projections and ego ideals we buy into. So let's tell ourselves some better mantras right now, mmkay?

**You don't need to be perfect.**

If the Millenneagram teaches us anything, it's that perfect and good are different things: one is a fantasy, and the other is attainable. The best good that you're capable of is to be your true self, your essence. Give her the space to thrive in your world, and watch as she makes decisions and creates relationships and says words that are both deeply true and deeply compassionate.

**You don't need to be nicer.**

Some of you have spent your lives trying to say less and need less and ask for less. Enough, now, honey. There isn't shit you can do to be respectable enough or small enough. Self-effacement is not an attainable goal! Knock that shit right the fuck off.

**You don't need to be harder.**

I know the world has been coming at you hard and fast forever. I know you feel like the walls you've built are the only things keeping the waves of trauma and suffering and heartbreak from bowling you clean the fuck over. I'm not telling you to tear them down. Just hollow us out a peephole maybe? Like the love of my life Lin-Manuel Miranda (whose tweets are literally the primary decorative motif in my apartment) tweets: "Build us a bridge to where you are."[1] Reject the message that strength is found only in boldness and bluster. It takes a lot of fucking nerve to be tender in a world like ours.

---

1. Lin-Manuel Miranda, Twitter feed, July 6, 2016, 5:21 a.m., https://twitter.com /lin_manuel/status/750666094164180993?lang=en.

# THE ENNEAGRAM AS AN INSTRUMENT
# OF SELF-HEALING

Here's the secret sauce of the Enneagram: it reminds you that you're exactly the way you're supposed to be. You might lean heavy on the neuroses at times (looking at you, Sixes) or you might be a grade-A drama queen (you know who you are, Fours), but you're authentically yourself. I know this is hard to believe for those of us coming from conservative, evangelical, or patriarchal cultures—ya know, those button-the-top-button kinda folks—but anything you have to force is not right or healthy or good. You should not have to force wholeness. Positive change should not look like white knuckles. It shouldn't look like repression. It shouldn't look like stifling or coping or self-flagellation. All of that behavior modification does nothing to actually change you long-term. All it does is mold you in the likeness of whatever deity the powers that be have constructed. Your adherence to the code of conduct set up for you and the roles you've been assigned does nothing but comfort the powerful, and not to sound like a full-blown fucking anarchist, but, like, they don't get to tell you who to be or how.

Listen, I'm not telling you what to believe (other than in the goodness of your own heart and the value of the people who surround you), but let's just run with that whole Divine Benevolent Being thing for a minute. Do you really believe that a Divine Benevolent Being who is all-powerful, all-knowing, and good would want you to erase yourself, with all your beautiful and strange and iridescent nuance, just so you look and behave and live the exact same life as someone else? Do you really think you exist only to reject your urges and dreams? Honestly, what would be the point of you being born so wildly unique, just to be tamed and homogenized and beaten down to size? I'm not buying that shit, and I don't think our benevolent deity would either. Sorry 'bout it.

The Enneagram was a huge part of my own healing. As you can tell, the church I grew up in left some scars, and it was ultimately the Enneagram that gave me a path to becoming the best person I could be in a way my religion just couldn't. When I was growing up in the church, there was this word they talked a lot about from the pulpit that meant "getting better," and that word was "sanctification." This word drove me nuts because I wanted to "get better," but the definition was vague as fuck: the only kind of answers I could get out of anybody were to be more "Christ-like" or practice the "fruits of the spirit," which basically meant "kindness" and "joy" and "peace." Those are easy to talk about and a fuck-ton harder to attain. My question was always "How do *I* PERSONALLY get there?" With the Enneagram's path to integration, I now feel like there's hope for my garbage ass. It's hard work, but I can become a kinder person. A more joyful person. A better person.

My friend Lacey, a One and steeped in evangelicalism herself, says this about trying to navigate her life prior to the Enneagram:

The hardest part of being in relationship with others is the fact that people don't live up to expectations of what they should do or be. I spent the first nine and a half years of my marriage trying to get my husband to fit into the box of a stereotypical evangelical man, but it didn't work and he refused to fit into that box. He was never interested in being the head of the household, making all the decisions, or telling me what to do. During that time I also tried to make myself into the good evangelical woman I should be. That didn't work either. I'm not interested in being a stay-at-home mom, writing in prayer journals, and blindly following my husband.

Trying to force us to be what we were "supposed" to be almost ruined everything. Finding the Enneagram saved us. Now I am able to accept and embrace the Nine traits in my husband, and he accepts and embraces the One traits in me. Now we have partnership.

Whatever the culture from which you hail, there's a good chance there are traditions and expectations you're meant to adhere to in order to maintain your Good Person badge. I know you've accepted that thing as a replacement for breathing, a consolation prize for not living your truth. But try this on for size: Maybe the idea of who should be getting Good Person badges has a lot more to do with traditions and systems of control and a lot less with the actual net good you're producing in the world. Maybe there's no one right way to be a good person, and maybe there's no advisory board signing off on who does and does not deserve badges.

## HEALING A DUMPSTER FIRE WORLD

If you follow me on Twitter, you know I'm not much of a kumbayah singer or high-road taker (forgive me, Michelle Obama!). I believe the liberal American understanding of peace is a peace that is cut off at the knees—one that values civility and respectability over truth and justice—and that is extremely not my shit. BUT. There is nothing more powerful than understanding one another to foment a culture of compassion and connectedness, and the Enneagram is one tool in our toolbox that can help us better understand our peers and even our frenemies. I believe we can approach activism or general revolutionary behavior only with a deep self-knowing, and with Millenneagram we can invite others to do the same.

This may be a grand-scale kinda dream, but I truly believe that men and women and nonbinary folks living out of their truest selves will make policies and raise families and stand up to power with a presence and a groundedness they would not otherwise be able to find.

## INTEGRATION AND COMING HOME
## TO YOURSELF

As my first fave band Relient K (I know, dude, step off) said in their song *Forward Motion*, "I struggle with forward motion," and got-dang, if that ain't all of us. Integration is terrifying because it challenges us to step outside the bounds of our egos, to open the door and embark on an adventure unlike any we have ever taken. Lucky for you, the Enneagram is a hella good map. For the first time maybe ever, you get to know what it will actually look like for you to rechart your course. To reimagine your relationships and the vicious cycles you can probably see woven through them. To know what you're shooting for.

Your ego is gonna be pissed about all this, just FYI. Don't expect that bitch to go quietly into the night. She has spent your whole life constructing your identity around a cheap-ass imitation of your true self and your real power. She's gonna pitch a fit when you begin recharting. Your instinct will be to shut her up or run away or avoid her like the fucking plague she feels like, but I challenge you to hear her out without judgment. Be present. Not to be alarmist, but that bitch can smell fear.

You will come to a moment—after you, and only you, have decided you are enough—when it will be time to retire the old scripts. You have written a beautiful survival story. There were always pieces of your true self in the old chapters. If you read back through, you can see the moments when she peeked out to see if she was welcome, and usually retreated when she realized she wasn't. Your brain ruts and personality ledges have all played pivotal roles in your story this far, and I would take this time to thank them. They got you here, and I'm grateful they did. You should be too. It's time to send them off in style, without judgment and without shame. Parade those motherfuckers onto some wispy white boats like angsty old Frodo at the end of *The Return of the King* and send them on their merry way. Tell them you've got this, and you've got new chapters to write.

Ya done good, kid. Doesn't that feel lighter now?

Once the old script is gone, it's time to get reacquainted with yourself. The you at your core, your true self, is maybe someone you haven't met before. Perhaps you have, but you're hardly old and dear friends yet. My mom used to call her little circle of BFFs the "back-door friends," which doesn't mean the dirty thing you're thinking of, gutter-brain. It means that the people you love get to come in the back door. No pomp, no circumstance, no ceremony. You gotta become your own back-door friend, but that shit takes time! Coming home can be a rather long journey when you've never been there before. The light must slowly be revealed and all that.

## WRITING NEW STORIES

Somebody once gave me a great tip about oral sex that also applies to both writing and self-growth. HEAR ME OUT. The original line was "You just gotta stay in the pussy," and for writing, I adapted it to "You just gotta stay on the page." For you then, the advice goes like this: "You just gotta stay in the now." Integration is not about constant motion. Sometimes it's just about looking yourself in the eye and nonjudgmentally acknowledging everything you see, like a yogi. It is equal parts doing, marinating, and creating.

**Doing.** Integration requires right action. It means taking back the reins of your life from your personality and being like *Nah, bitch, this is \*my\* job now.* It means doing the right thing when you know it's the right thing, instead of letting fear and indecision cause you to lose out on opportunities that life brings around only one time. Again, not choosing is a choice too. Whatever you have not done in the past is ancient history, though, boo. You only have today. This is the only day you can show up for.

**Marinating.** You gotta lot of years to catch up on with yourself, babe. Your ego shields you from potential harm, but it also shields you from yourself. Once you start to see and feel your essence, marinate in that shit. Repeat your truth over and over to yourself, like a mantra. Like a liturgy. You've been living off survival stories. It's time to write a new kind. Resetting all your default knee-jerks and all the emotional bones that have healed crooked takes time and repetition, and it's not the sort of thing one should attempt alone. The good thing is that you aren't, and neither am I.

**Creating.** You are the captain and cartographer of a better future. You are laying the sod and planting the seeds in a new emotional landscape. Go ham on that shit. Your true self is an adventure worth taking.

Capitalism teaches us that self-love is about the things we buy ourselves, the vacations we take, the money we spend and make. The culture of self-help tells us that we should be and should want to be richer, happier, skinnier, and more famous. Even the better, more progressive shit out there tells us that we have to be blanket-statement vulnerable, just laying ourselves at the feet of the world and daring it to do its worst to us. All that shit is ancillary to the subtle but gargantuan task of showing up for ourselves. We are our longest and dearest relationship. We cannot be fully seen and fully known by anyone else if we cannot fully see and fully know ourselves.

For the first time, maybe ever, you get to work on yourself without adhering to anybody else's expectations for what you should look like or how you should behave or how you should turn out. Nobody fucking knows this shit but you, friend! You are the expert on you! All of this information I just threw at you is a starting point—a launching pad. You get to go deep diving now and see what you come up with. Maybe you took a test and thought you were one number, and the more you dig and consider, compare and contrast, you realize you're another. Girl, that is FINE. What your Enneagram number should never do is pin you down. It's not static. That's like saying the Constitution can't be amended! It has been, and let's be honest, it needs plenty more.

Get your ass on the page, and sit there until what needs to come out does. It's usually not this glamorous epiphany moment. You might come to yourself while you're ordering a soy white mocha in a pretentious coffee shop. Sometimes self-discovery is boring. Like *Damn, girl, you did that shit AGAIN? Guess we gotta figure out why!* Sometimes it's like walking in the back door of a house that seems familiar, like a place you wandered into in your dreams. Sometimes it just means crying until you can't anymore. Get it out honey . . . but stay on the page.

You are a living document, and so is your life. Get to writing.

As Riso and Hudson say, you are invited to ABUNDANCE.

As *I* tell you now, you are invited to believe that your value is not in the mistakes you don't make.

You are invited to believe that you need shit, and it's okay to ask for it.

You are invited to believe that your feelings are valid and your identity is yours to build.

You are invited to believe that belonging is real and happiness is attainable.

You are invited to believe that you have what it takes to be a competent human in the world.

You are invited to believe that you are the source of your security. You are your own safety net.

You are invited to believe that your joy is meaningful and needed.

You are invited to believe that you can be both powerful and tender at once.

You are invited to believe that your opinion matters.

You are invited to believe that you

are the point

of you.

Will you accept the invitation?

Check out some other cool shit about the Enneagram and becoming your true self.

**MY BIBLE**

*The Wisdom of the Enneagram: The Complete Guide to Psychological and Spiritual Growth for the Nine Personality Types*, Don Richard Riso and Russ Hudson

**STARS IN THE ENNEAGRAM CONSTELLATION**

*Personality Types: Using the Enneagram for Self-Discovery*, Don Richard Riso and Russ Hudson

*The Enneagram of Passions and Virtues: Finding the Way Home*, Sandra Maitri

*The Complete Enneagram: 27 Paths to Greater Self-Knowledge*, Beatrice Chestnut

*The Sacred Enneagram: Finding Your Unique Path to Spiritual Growth*, Chris Heuertz

*The Enneagram in Love & Work: Understanding Your Intimate & Business Relationships*, Helen Palmer

*The Enneagram: A Christian Perspective*, Richard Rohr and Andreas Ebert

## ADDITIONAL WHOLENESS AND HEALING SHIT

*The Body Keeps the Score: Integration of Mind, Brain, and Body in the Treatment of Trauma*, Bessel A. van der Kolk

*Trauma Stewardship: An Everyday Guide to Caring for Self While Caring for Others*, Laura van Dernoot Lipsky with Connie Burk

*Wounded Heart: Hope for Adult Victims of Childhood Sexual Abuse*, Dan B. Allender

*The Drama of the Gifted Child*, Alice Miller (Ya kinda won't go wrong reading anything this woman has written.)

## SOMETHING ABSOLUTELY EVERYONE SHOULD READ AND IMPLEMENT REGARDLESS OF PROFESSION

*The Artist's Way*, Julia Cameron

Make sure to check out Sleeping at Last's gorgeous collection of Enneagram-based songs in his Atlas series. You know what? While you're at it, just listen to every damn song the man (Ryan O'Neal) has ever released.

## ACKNOWLEDGMENTS

To the readers & tweeters & patrons & mug-buyers of Millennea-gram, it all started with you. I couldn't have done any of this shit without you.

To the queer, feminist, and anti-racist activists who have both taught me & let me listen.

To Moody fucking Bible Institute, for radicalizing a bitch.

To Josh Puckett, for always helping a bitch out of troubled water from far away.

To Corey (@coreypigg), my producer & my friend, for believing in me before I did.

To Kevin Garcia (@thekevingarcia), Stacey Midge (@revstacey), Jamie Lee Finch (@jamielee finch), Anna Skates (@anna_skates), Eli Nichols, Laura Jean Truman, & countless others who lent their voices to these pages. These are the folks you listen to. Check them out on Twitter.

To Annalisa Webb, Michael Vasquez, Tori Douglass, Melissa Hawks, Bethany & Matt Suckrow, Sueann Shiah, Hannah Schaefer, Ashley Blum, Melissa Greene, Jameson Savage, and Jenny Bones for inspiring me with your passion & your wisdom & your small & tall tales.

To the QFDT—y'all know who you are. Fictive kin yo.

To Mom and Dad, who are my genesis story. I am who I am because of you.

To Amy, Maria, Nathan, Courtney, Emily, and Billy—we made friends into family. Thank you for holding me.

To Josh & Rebecca, for finding me.

To my body, for loving me even when I didn't know how to love her. We did this, you & me.

PHOTOGRAPH BY NICOLETTE LOVELL

**HANNAH PAASCH** is the blogger, podcast host, and Twitter influencer behind #millenneagram. She also is credited with starting the #churchtoo movement, drawing attention to sexual misconduct within places of worship. She has been featured in *Jezebel*, *Religion & Politics*, ABC, *Vox*, *America*, *Bustle*, *Teen Vogue*, *TIME*, *Mother Jones*, *HelloGiggles*, and more.

HannahPaasch  |  @HannahPaasch  |  HannahPaasch.com

**235**